SEWING BIBLE
CURTAINS

SERIES EDITOR **WENDY GARDINER**

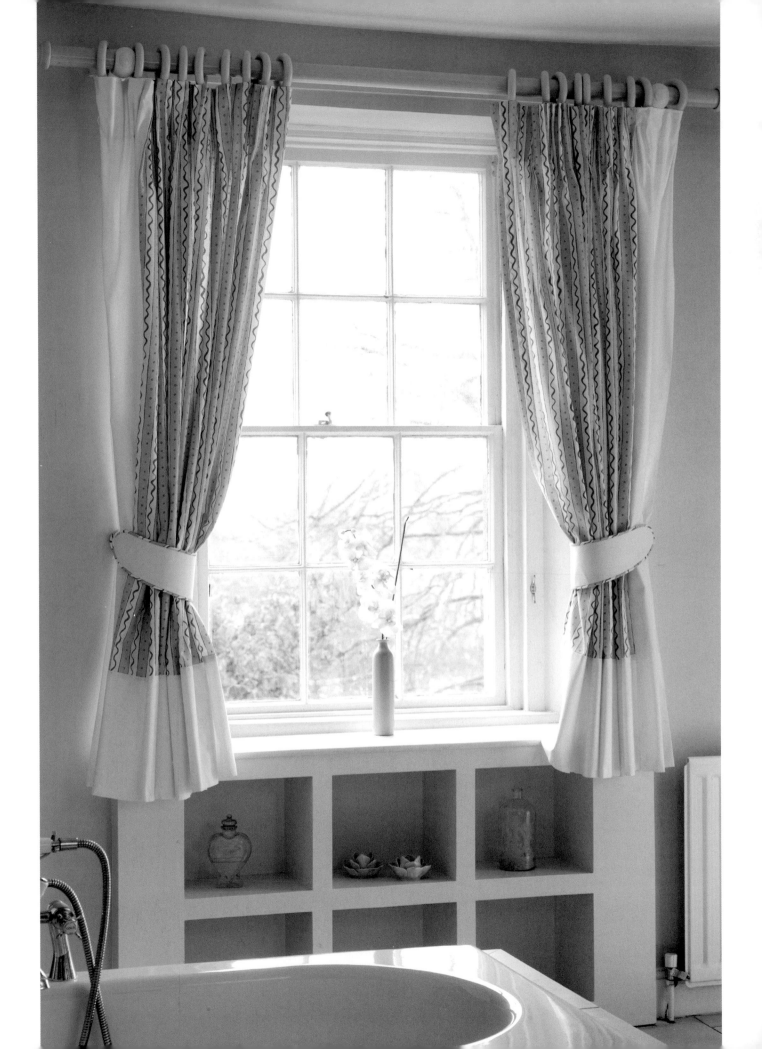

SEWING BIBLE
CURTAINS

SERIES EDITOR **WENDY GARDINER**

A DAVID & CHARLES BOOK
Copyright © David & Charles Limited 2009

David & Charles is an F+W Media Inc. company
4700 East Galbraith Road
Cincinnati, OH 45236

First published in the UK in 2009

Text and designs copyright © Wendy Gardiner 2009
Photography © David & Charles 2009

A catalogue record for this book is available from the British Library.

ISBN-13: 978-0-7153-3041-8 paperback
ISBN-10: 0-7153-3041-1 paperback

Printed in China by RR Donnelley
for David & Charles
Brunel House   Newton Abbot   Devon

Commissioning Editor: Jennifer Fox-Proverbs
Editor: Bethany Dymond
Assistant Editor: Kate Nicholson
Project Editor: Karen Hemingway
Senior Design Director: Prudence Rogers
Art Editor: Sarah Clark
Senior Designer: Sarah Underhill
Production Controllers: Beverley Richardson and Alison Smith
Photographer: Simon Whitmore

Visit our website at www.davidandcharles.co.uk

David & Charles books are available from all good bookshops;
alternatively you can contact our Orderline on 0870 9908222 or write
to us at FREEPOST EX2 110, D&C Direct, Newton Abbot, TQ12 4ZZ
(no stamp required UK only); US customers call 800-289-0963 and
Canadian customers call 800-840-5220.

CONTENTS

Introduction

UPDATING WINDOW TREATMENTS IS A QUICK WAY TO REVAMP A ROOM AND, AS CURTAINS ARE ONE OF THE EASIEST TYPES OF SOFT FURNISHING TO MAKE, THEY ARE ALSO A GREAT WAY TO ADD PERSONAL STYLE OR COMPLEMENT A COLOUR SCHEME. ALTHOUGH CURTAINS OFTEN INVOLVE LARGE PIECES OF FABRIC, THEY HAVE SIMPLE SHAPES, FEW PIECES TO ASSEMBLE AND ARE GENERALLY SEWN WITH STRAIGHT SEAMS, SO YOU DON'T NEED TO BE AN EXPERIENCED SEWER TO ACHIEVE PROFESSIONAL RESULTS.

TEAM THE GORGEOUS FABRICS AVAILABLE, WITH EASY-TO-USE HEADER TAPES, POLES AND TIEBACKS, AND YOU CAN QUICKLY UPDATE YOUR DÉCOR AND HAVE THE SATISFACTION OF KNOWING YOU ACHIEVED THE LOOK YOURSELF.

THIS BOOK INCLUDES ALL THE BASIC INFORMATION REQUIRED TO GET STARTED, EXPLAINING THE EQUIPMENT YOU NEED AND PROBABLY HAVE ALREADY, HOW TO MEASURE WINDOWS AND CHOOSE FABRICS, AS WELL AS HOW TO MASTER THE BASIC TECHNIQUES. THE FOLLOWING 12 CHAPTERS HAVE MORE IN-DEPTH INFORMATION ON THE TECHNIQUES USED TO ACHIEVE A WIDE VARIETY OF WINDOW TREATMENTS. EACH CHAPTER ALSO FEATURES A STUNNING PROJECT EXPLAINED IN STEP-BY-STEP INSTRUCTIONS AND CLEAR ILLUSTRATIONS.

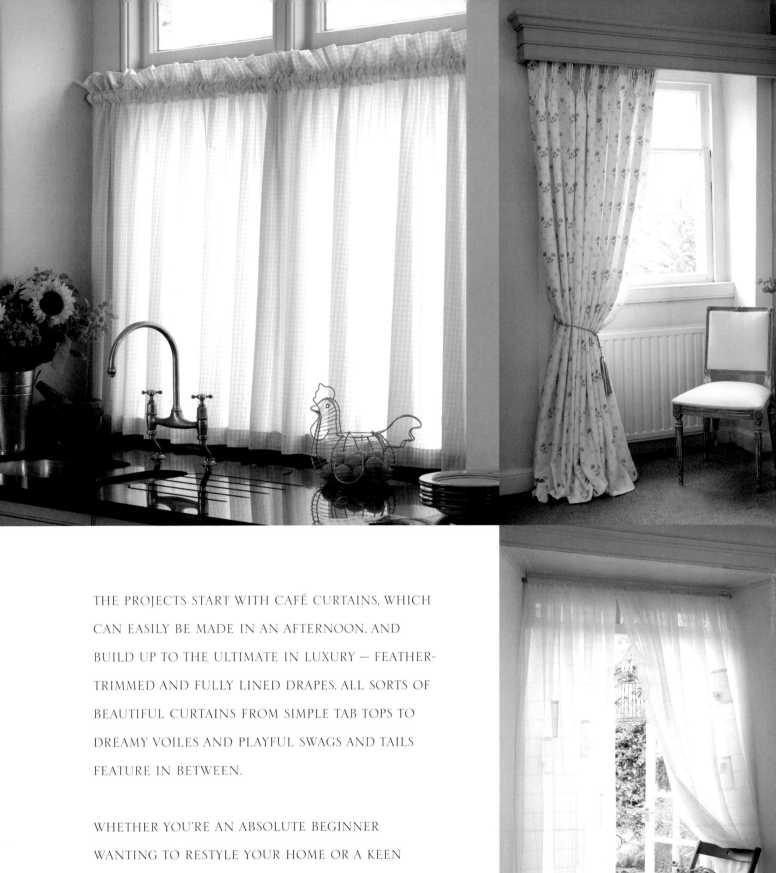

THE PROJECTS START WITH CAFÉ CURTAINS, WHICH
CAN EASILY BE MADE IN AN AFTERNOON, AND
BUILD UP TO THE ULTIMATE IN LUXURY — FEATHER-
TRIMMED AND FULLY LINED DRAPES. ALL SORTS OF
BEAUTIFUL CURTAINS FROM SIMPLE TAB TOPS TO
DREAMY VOILES AND PLAYFUL SWAGS AND TAILS
FEATURE IN BETWEEN.

WHETHER YOU'RE AN ABSOLUTE BEGINNER
WANTING TO RESTYLE YOUR HOME OR A KEEN
SEWER LOOKING FOR NEW IDEAS, SEWING BIBLE.
CURTAINS HAS SOMETHING FOR YOU.

HAVE FUN SEWING!

BASIC EQUIPMENT

TO MAKE CURTAINS SUCCESSFULLY, ALL YOU NEED ARE A FEW ITEMS OF BASIC EQUIPMENT, WHICH YOU WILL PROBABLY ALREADY HAVE IN YOUR SEWING KIT. ARMED WITH THESE, YOU WILL BE READY TO TACKLE ALL TYPES OF WINDOW TREATMENT WITH CONFIDENCE.

MAKE SURE YOU KEEP YOUR EQUIPMENT IN THE BEST CONDITION SO THAT YOU CAN PRODUCE REALLY PROFESSIONAL RESULTS. ALWAYS INVEST IN THE BEST QUALITY YOU CAN AFFORD AND, IF YOU ARE TEMPTED, THERE ARE VARIOUS ADDITIONAL TOOLS AVAILABLE THAT WILL SAVE YOU TIME AND EFFORT.

BASIC SEWING KIT

This kit is recommended for making all your curtains, including the projects in this book. You will find more detail on which types to choose on the following pages.

✓ Sewing machine and needles
✓ Shears and scissors
✓ Long, glass-headed pins
✓ Marking tool
✓ General-purpose thread
✓ Tape measure, metre (yard) stick, set square

SEWING MACHINE

Although you can, of course, sew by hand, it is far quicker to make curtains with a sewing machine. A basic machine with straight and zigzag stitch is all that is needed. Make sure your machine is in good working order and that you have a good understanding of how it works, using the manufacturer's manual for guidance. You will need various feet and a selection of needles to use with your machine.

ZIP FOOT   BLIND HEM FOOT   WALKING FOOT

SEWING MACHINE FEET

The **general purpose** or **straight stitch foot** is the basic foot that comes with the machine and is suitable for all general purposes such as sewing seams.

A **zipper foot** is useful for piping as well as for inserting zippers. It usually has a thinner centre with grooves either side so that you can stitch close to the zipper teeth or piping cord.

A **walking foot** will help feed the top and bottom fabrics evenly as you sew. This is particularly useful for pattern matching and when sewing thick plush fabrics such as fleece or velvet.

A **blind hem foot** often has a thin metal strip extending below the foot, which is used to butt against the folded hem. The blind hemstitch, found on most modern sewing machines, will stitch straight stitch within the hem allowance and a regularly spaced but occasional zigzag stitch into the main curtain, thus securing the hem in place. All that is visible from the right side of the fabric is a very tiny ladder stitch.

A BASIC SEWING MACHINE WITH STRAIGHT AND ZIGZAG STITCH IS ALL YOU REALLY NEED TO SEW CURTAINS SUCCESSFULLY.

MACHINE NEEDLES

When sewing most soft furnishing fabrics, choose a robust needle: sizes 12–14 (80–90 European) for medium-weight fabrics and sizes 16–18 (100–110) for heavyweight fabrics. For very heavy fabrics, use a size 20 (120) needle. For lightweight voiles, a size 9–11 (60–75) is suitable.

Remember to change the needle with every new project. A blunt needle can cause skipped stitches, broken thread and even holes or snags in the fabric. Always have a supply of spare needles to hand so that you can replace broken needles quickly.

EXPERT TIP

IF A SEAM PUCKERS, THE NEEDLE MAY BE TOO BIG, SO TRY A SMALLER ONE. IF THE NEEDLE OR THREAD BREAKS, THE NEEDLE MAY BE TOO SMALL, SO TRY A BIGGER ONE.

SHARP, GOOD QUALITY DRESSMAKING SHEARS AND LONG PINS ARE ESSENTIALS ITEMS OF KIT.

SCISSORS

Dressmaking shears

You can recognise shears by the moulded handles, the larger hole for your hand and a smaller one for your thumb. They are available for right- and left-handed use, with the moulded handles appropriately shaped. Make sure your shears are good quality with long straight blades so you can cut smoothly. Keep the blades sharp and never use them for anything other than cutting fabric.

Some dressmaking shears have very fine serrated edges along the cutting blades, which help to grip the fabric as it is cut. Others have soft-touch handles that are slightly spongy and useful if you are cutting large quantities at a time because they are gentler on the hand. Spring-loaded scissors, with handles one on top of the other, are also available. They spring open between cuts, making them easier to use if your hands suffer from arthritis.

Dressmaking scissors

A pair of dressmaking scissors is handy for clipping into seam allowances, cutting threads and also cutting smaller curves and notches.

Seam rippers

Also known as quick-unpicks, these often come with sewing machines. They have a hooked blade with a pointed end, which is slipped under stitches and pushed through to cut the thread. They are also very handy for cutting open buttonholes. Take care to use a seam ripper in a controlled manner and ensure that you are not cutting anything you did not anticipate.

Rotary cutters

A rotary cutter has a circular blade attached to a handle. It must be used on a cutting mat, and a long cutting ruler is also useful. Cutters can simply be rolled along a cutting line to cut through fabric and are ideal for large projects with straight edges. Some cutters have blades that can be safely retracted when not in use or alternative blades with different cutting effects such as fluted edges. Remember that the sharp cutter is a potential hazard and store it safely.

PINKING SHEARS

These have serrated edges and make a zigzag cut to fabric, which helps to prevent the fabric fraying. They can be used to neatened edges of lightweight cottons and poly/cotton fabrics quickly and easily. They are also useful for cutting interfacing.

PINS

Long glass-headed or flower-headed pins are ideal for making soft furnishings. Place them at right angles to the seam so they can be removed easily as you sew. Replace blunt pins regularly to avoid them snagging fabric. Remember that should they come into contact with heat, from an iron for example, any plastic heads on pins will melt. You could also use quilting safety pins for pinning layers of fabric together.

SEWING SENSE

When cutting out delicate fabrics that might be marked by pins, use fabric weights (or even clean tin cans) instead of pins to stop the fabric shifting.

THREADS

Use a good quality general-purpose polyester-covered cotton thread for most projects. Of course, you can opt to use silk threads on delicate silk fabrics and pure cotton thread with cotton or linen fabric. Choose a thread colour that matches the fabric. If you can't find an exact match, it is better to go slightly darker with the thread. For patterned fabric, match the background or most prominent colour. Allow two to three 110yd (100m) reels of thread for a pair of curtains, depending on the size of the curtains.

MEASURING TOOLS

A good quality **tape measure** is essential. One that shows metric and imperial measurements on the same side is ideal.

Easier for long lengths, a straight **metre (yard) stick** can be used to measure and mark curtain lengths quickly.

An accurate large **set square**, such as a carpenters' square, is ideal for giving you a perfect right angle. The two rulers or outer edges will help you ensure that fabric is straight both vertically (lengthwise) and horizontally (crosswise).

A **French curve** is a curved measuring tool, which is very useful for marking out and drawing curves. They are either a length of bendy plastic or a flat, hard plastic shape with different curved areas and markings.

MARKING TOOLS

A selection of marking tools is useful. They all have different advantages, so choose the type to suit your project and a colour to show up on your fabric.

Chalk markers are convenient to use because chalk is easily removed once it has served its purpose. They are available in different forms. A **chalk wheel** deposits a very fine line of loose chalk as you run the wheel along the line to be marked. Different colours of loose chalk are available in pre-packed containers. **Chalk pencils** usually come in packs of two colours, white and pink or blue, to use on light or dark fabric. Some are propelling pencils with tubes of different coloured chalk. A **chalk block**, contained in a plastic case, has a sharp edge so you can draw lines and make marks easily.

Marker pens come in a wide variety from permanent markers to water- or air-soluble pens. Vanishing or fade-away pens and pencils will fade after about 48 hours, so avoid using them if you plan to make a project over an extended period! Water-soluble pens are usually blue and the marks can be removed with a damp sponge or by washing. Do check how easily they are removed by checking on a scrap of fabric first.

INTERFACING AND INTERLINING

Occasionally you may wish to add interfacing or interlining to a curtain to give it more body and greater strength. Interfacing is often used at the header for tab-top curtains or for those that do not use a header tape.

Pick an **interfacing** that suits the fabric being used. For instance, a medium-weight soft furnishing fabric will need a medium-weight interfacing. The idea is to add strength and stability without changing the handle of the fabric. There are sew-in and fusible varieties. **Sew-in interfacings** should be machine stitched to the wrong side of the fabric close to the edge all the way around.

Fusible interfacings are quick to use, but best avoided on fabrics with surface texture because you need to press well, which might flatten the surface of the fabric. Always press them to the wrong side of the fabric, lowering the iron onto the interfacing and pressing with a hot dry iron. Hold the iron in place for at least 10 seconds before lifting it off, moving to the next section and lowering it again. Do not glide the iron until the interfacing is securely in place. Once it is, allow the fabrics to cool before handling them again.

EXPERT TIP

CUT INTERFACING WITH PINKING SHEARS TO AVOID A PRONOUNCED HARD LINE.

Interlining is simply another layer of fabric, used to add bulk, weight and stability to the main fabric. It will also add richness to curtain fullness and help long curtains hang well. It can be a lining fabric, cotton muslin or simply a toning lightweight cotton. Cut it to the same size as the main fabric and sew them wrong sides together around the edges, ready to work with both layers as one.

HANDY ACCESSORIES

A **point turner** looks like a short ruler, with one end angled to a point, which is used to push out corners fully. The measurements on the ruler also make this tool useful for accurately measuring and marking hems and side turnings.

A good quality steam **iron** is essential for any sewing project. When pressing, especially a delicate fabric or one with surface detail, always use a **pressing cloth** to protect the fabric. An ideal cloth is silk organza, which can withstand high temperatures and is transparent so you can see exactly what you are pressing.

EXPERT TIP

TO AVOID CRUSHING THE PILE ON A PLUSH FABRIC, USE A REMNANT OF THE SAME FABRIC AS A PRESSING CLOTH, PLACING THE TWO PILE TO PILE.

A **serger** is a very useful piece of equipment to own because it sews the seams, cuts off the seam allowance and overlocks the edges in one pass. Machines use from three to eight threads. However, a good pair of shears and the zigzag stitch on your sewing machine make sure that you achieve results that are just as serviceable.

BASIC TECHNIQUES

THERE ARE A FEW BASIC STITCHES AND SEWING TECHNIQUES THAT ARE HANDY TO KNOW BEFORE STARTING ON SOFT FURNISHINGS. THESE INCLUDE SOME GENERAL-PURPOSE HAND STITCHES, SIMPLE MACHINE STITCHING AND TECHNIQUES FOR SEAMING, NEATENING EDGES, TOP STITCHING AND HEMMING.

HAND STITCHING

The most useful hand stitches are basting, hemming, slip stitch and blind hemstitch. Armed with these basics, you are ready to tackle any project.

BASTING

Basting is a way of temporarily holding together two or more layers of fabric with either thread or pins. Pins can be removed more quickly as you sew, but thread will hold the layers more securely.

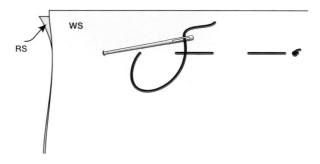

FIGURE 1 BASTING STITCHES ARE TEMPORARY AND WILL BE REMOVED LATER

When thread basting, use a thread that contrasts with the fabric so it is easy to see and remove later. Make a knot at one end of the thread and start sewing at one end of the seam. Make long running stitches, of even length, through the layers of fabric, along the seam line.

Alternatively, you can also use large basted cross stitches to hold the lining and main fabric together before stitching them permanently.

Once the permanent seam is stitched, remove the basting thread by cutting the knot and pulling the thread out. If a long row of basting stitches has been made, snip the thread at regular intervals along the seam before pulling it out.

SEWING SENSE

The diagrams in this book use the following abbreviations for quick reference:
C – centre
RS – right side of the fabric
SA – seam allowance
WS – wrong side of the fabric

To pin baste, insert the pins through the layers of fabric at right angles to the seam so they can be removed as you sew. On small projects, place pins 1–3in (2.5–7.5cm) apart. On large projects, such as curtains, space them every 4–8in (10–15cm).

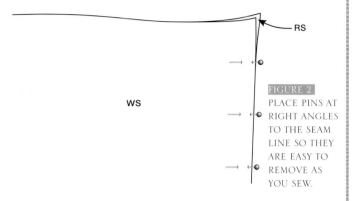

SEWING SENSE

Side and bottom hems on curtains are usually double hems. Turn the raw edge under and press. Turn the folded edge under again, and press, to make a double hem.

SLIP STITCH

FIGURE 3
TAKE TINY STITCHES INTO THE MAIN FABRIC, PICKING UP JUST ONE OR TWO THREADS, SO THE STITCHES ARE VIRTUALLY INVISIBLE.

Slip stitch is used to hem lightweight fabrics. Small stitches are taken so that they are virtually invisible on the right side once the hem is stitched.
1 Secure the end of the thread within the folds of the hem.
2 Slip the needle through just one or two fibres of the main fabric and then up through the hem fold at a slight angle to the left. Pull the thread through.
3 Repeat this process to the end of the hem, keeping the stitches and tension even.

BLIND HEMMING

FIGURE 4 WORK BLIND HEMMING IN THE SAME WAY AS SLIP STITCH.

The effects of blind hemming are very similar to slip stitching, but the technique is more suitable for heavier weight fabrics. It prevents an unsightly ridge showing on the right side along the top edge of the hem.

Turn down the folded hem allowance and stitch in the same way as for slip stitching, taking up one or two fibres of main fabric before catching the turned under hem allowance. Repeat along the hem.

HERRINGBONE STITCH

This stitch is particularly usefully for securing side hems. It should not be pulled too tight so it does not pucker the fabric.
1 Work from left to right on the wrong side. Secure the thread end in the folded edge of the hem, bringing the needle out through the hem.
2 Make a small stitch diagonally to the right, inserting the needle horizontally from right to left through the main fabric.
3 Make a second small stitch as before, but this time in the hem fabric. Continue in the same way to the end of the hem.

FIGURE 5 WORK HERRINGBONE STITCH FROM LEFT TO RIGHT.

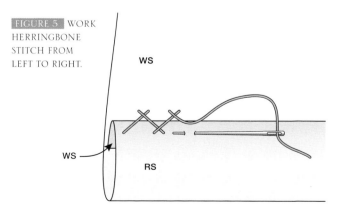

LOCK STITCH

This is a useful stitch for hemming. Because each stitch is locked individually, the hem will not unravel if threads break, which means only a small area needs repairing.

1 Using a small needle, secure the thread end in the folded edge of the hem.

2 Working from right to left, pick up one or two fibres from the main curtain fabric and bring the needle up through the folded hem allowance directly below.

3 Pull the thread until it is almost through and then take the needle, from right to left, under the long loop of thread. Pull through to form a lock stitch.

FIGURE 6 MAKE SURE YOU KEEP AN EVEN TENSION WHEN PULLING THE THREAD THROUGH.

4 Continue, making evenly spaced lock stitches, approximately 1in (2.5cm) apart, along the length of the hem.

EXPERT TIP
THE FURTHER APART THE LOCK STITCHES ARE, THE LESS VISIBLE THEY WILL BE ON THE RIGHT SIDE OF THE FABRIC.

LADDER STITCH

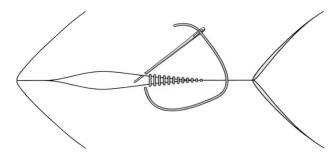

FIGURE 7 PULL THE STITCHES UP AS YOU SEW.

This stitch is used to close relatively short openings, such as those left for turning items like cushion covers and pockets tops

through to the right side, or for attaching trims by hand. Like slip stitch and blind hemming, it is almost invisible to see once the stitches are pulled up.

1 First press the seam allowance on both sides of the opening so that the edges butt perfectly.

2 Secure the thread in the seam allowance and bring the needle to the right side through the fold on one side of the seam.

3 Take a small stitch through the opposite edge of the seam, coming out a short distance along the seam.

4 Now take a small stitch in the first edge of the seam, starting opposite the end of the previous stitch and coming out a short distance along the seam.

5 Continue, gently pulling the thread to close the opening as you sew, until the opening is fully closed.

PRICK STITCH

This stitch is used to insert a zipper by hand or give a decorative top-stitched edge. A row of tiny stitches are visible on the right side so you could use a contrasting colour of thread.

1 Secure the thread on the wrong side of the fabric and then bring the needle to the right side. Take a tiny stitch backwards along the seam line, down to the wrong side.

2 Bring the needle up to the right side again approximately ¼in (6mm) along the seam line to the left, ready to make the next back stitch.

FIGURE 8 PRICK STITCH CREATES A LINE OF TINY STITCHES ON THE RIGHT SIDE WITH LONG RUNNING STITCHES ON THE BACK.

SEWING SENSE
Using chalk pencil, mark a stitch line on the wrong side of the fabric to make sure your stitches stay in a straight row.

GATHERING STITCH

A gathering stitch can be used to gather fabric or ease in a seam. You can gently ease the fullness of a small amount of fabric, for instance on curved hems, so that no visible gathers can be seen on the right side. The smaller the stitches, the smaller the gathers.

1 Secure a double thread on the seam line. To gather, make long running stitches, of even length, through the layers of fabric, along the seam line. You can easily take three or four stitches at a time. To ease, sew within the seam allowance instead.

FIGURE 9 TAKE THREE OR FOUR STITCHES AT A TIME TO SEW GATHERING STITCH MORE QUICKLY.

2 When you reach the end of the seam line, pull the thread tails up to gather or ease the fabric as much as required.
3 To secure the threads and keep the fabric gathered, wrap the thread ends around a vertically placed pin. Alternatively, stitch on the spot to secure thread.
4 Distribute the gathers evenly along the length of fabric or ease the fabric around the curve.

SEWING SENSE

When sewing, always keep as much of the fabric to the left of your machine as possible. This means that the raw edges of a seam, for example, will run to the right side of the needle in the machine.

MACHINE STITCHING

The most commonly used machine stitches for making curtains are straight stitch and zigzag or overcast stitch. The straight stitch is used to sew regular straight seams and the zigzag or overcast is used to neaten raw edges on lined curtains where the seams will not be visible. Seams for curtains without linings are described on pp. 36–37 and those suitable for sheers are given on p. 81.

STRAIGHT STITCH

FIGURE 10 RUN THE MACHINE AT A MEDIUM SPEED TO SEW ACCURATELY STRAIGHT ALONG THE SEAM LINE.

Choose a stitch length to suit the fabric being sewn. Lightweight fabrics will need a shorter stitch length of 2.2–2.5; thicker fabrics will need longer stitches of 3–3.5 to prevent the fabric buckling and puckering or the thread breaking. To determine the best length, try straight stitching on remnants of the same fabric, remembering to use the same number of layers and any interfacing or header tape. A perfect stitch is perfectly tensioned, with the top thread on the top and the bobbin thread on the underside.

EXPERT TIP

STITCH CURTAIN PANELS TOGETHER FROM THE HEM EDGE TO THE TOP. IF THE PATTERN REPEAT GOES OUT OF ALIGNMENT, ANY DISCREPANCY WILL BE IN THE HEADER FOLDS AND THUS LESS VISIBLE.

TENSION

With most modern sewing machines, the needle tension is set for general-purpose sewing and doesn't need adjusting for making curtains. If, however, you do find that the needle thread is showing too much on the wrong side of the fabric, then very slightly increase the tension according to instructions in the manual. Test stitch on a remnant of the same fabric and number of layers as being used for project.

SEWING SEAMS

FIGURE 11 USE REVERSE STITCH TO STOP THE THREAD UNRAVELLING.

A regular straight seam can be used in many situations. It can be used in the techniques and projects in this book, unless another specific type of seam is recommended. (You will find other seams for specific purposes on pp. 36–37 and 81.)

Make sure that the thread is secured at the start and finish of a seam to prevent the stitching unravelling. The easiest method is to backstitch or reverse stitch at the beginning and end of the seam.

1 Holding both the bobbin and top threads behind the machine foot, stitch four or five stitches forward along the seam line. Stop and, pressing the reverse button, stitch back over the previous stitches. Now sew forward again to the other end of the seam.

2 Reverse stitch again over the last four or five stitches and then continue forward again to the end of seam.

3 Remove the work from the sewing machine, take the thread tails to the back of the work and trim them close to the fabric.

4 Press the seam, right sides together, to embed the stitches.

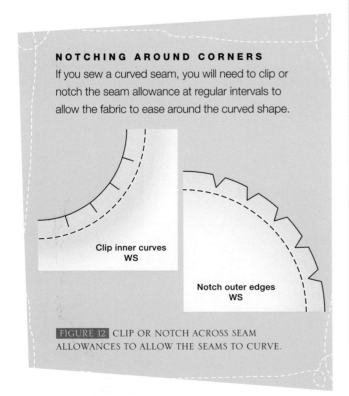

NOTCHING AROUND CORNERS

If you sew a curved seam, you will need to clip or notch the seam allowance at regular intervals to allow the fabric to ease around the curved shape.

Clip inner curves
WS

Notch outer edges
WS

FIGURE 12 CLIP OR NOTCH ACROSS SEAM ALLOWANCES TO ALLOW THE SEAMS TO CURVE.

SEWING SENSE

Always press a seam before stitching over it – once, with right sides together, to embed the stitches; then a second time, with the seam opened out, if you are making a flat seam.

MACHINE BASTING

This has the same function as hand basting, but is achieved by stitching on a machine, set to the longest stitch possible. Stitch without securing the thread at either end (i.e. without reverse stitching) and use a contrasting thread colour so that it is easy to see and remove later.

When you are ready to remove the basting, use scissors or a seam ripper to cut through the stitches at intervals and then pull out the thread tails.

NEATENING EDGES

SEWING SENSE

Use pinking shears to quickly neaten stable lightweight fabrics such as cottons.

Zigzag stitch

Overcast stitch

WS   WS

SA   RS

FIGURE 13 NEATEN EDGES TO STOP THE FABRIC FRAYING.

Raw fabric edges need to be neatened to prevent the fabric from fraying. Once the seam is pressed open, neaten each seam allowance by stitching a zigzag, or overcast stitch, close to the edges. Press the work again.

TOP STITCH

FIGURE 14 TOP STITCH TO HOLD A FACING OR HEM IN PLACE WITH A DECORATIVE FINISH.

This stitching shows on the surface of the fabric. It is used as a decorative finish as well as to hold facings and hems in place. You can choose to use decorative stitches or contrasting thread to make the stitching more of a feature. Although any thread can be used, a top-stitch thread is usually thicker and thus more easily visible. Thicker thread needs to be sewn with a larger-eyed needle and slightly longer stitch length of 3–3.5.

A machine-stitched hem is effectively top-stitched because it will show on the right side. However, if you want the stitching to virtually disappear into the fabric, choose a matching thread. Use a straight stitch and sew close to the top fold of the hem allowance to hold the hem neatly in place.

EDGE STITCH

This is an alternative to top stitching. It also shows on the right side of the fabric, but is sewn closer to the edge of the fabric.

TURNING A DOUBLE HEM

A double hem makes the perfect finish to the side and bottom edges of curtains. Simply turn the raw edge under once, and then again by the same amount. Press, and then stitch it in place by the desired method.

BLIND HEMMING

WS   RS

FIGURE 15 USE THE BLIND HEM FUNCTION ON YOUR MACHINE FOR AN INVISIBLE FINISH.

Hem allowance

This very useful machine-stitching technique enables you to hem curtains quickly and almost invisibly!

1 Fold the hem allowance under and neaten the raw edge or tuck it under again. Then fold the hem allowance back under the main fabric to leave just ½–1in (1.25–2.5cm) still showing (see the diagram above).

2 On your machine, select blind hem stitch, which produces a repeat pattern of a few straight stitches followed by one left swing zigzag.

3 Preferably use a blind hem foot, which usually has a thin metal strip protruding below the foot against which you should line up the folded fabric. The straight stitches go into the hem allowance only, with the zigzag swing to the left catching into the folded-back main fabric.

4 Once complete and with the hem allowance hanging properly, the only visible stitch on the right side of fabric is a tiny ladder stitch. However, if the thread matches the fabric closely, this will be virtually invisible.

STITCHING IN THE DITCH

This is a useful technique to master if you want to complete projects by machine and save time on hand stitching. Stitching in the ditch is a way of stitching from the right side in order to keep borders or bindings that are wrapped around to the underside in place on the wrong side.

1 Sew the binding or border to the main fabric, right sides together and with the raw edges matching.

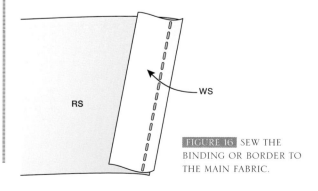

RS   WS

FIGURE 16 SEW THE BINDING OR BORDER TO THE MAIN FABRIC.

2 Trim the seam allowances to a scant ¼in (6mm). If stitching bulky fabric, grade the seam allowances by cutting one to ⅜in (1cm) and the other to ¼in (6mm) in order to reduce bulk.

FIGURE 17 TRIM THE SEAM ALLOWANCE TO REDUCE BULK.

3 Press the seam and then press the binding or border open, with the seam allowances towards the raw edge of the binding or border.

4 Fold the binding or border over the raw edges to the wrong side, pinning it in place so that the unattached edge covers the seam line.

5 Working from the right side, place the work under the machine foot so the needle will penetrate the previous seam line. As you stitch in the ditch, pull the seam apart slightly so the new stitches sink into the previous seam line. The underside of the binding or border will also be caught in place by the stitching.

FIGURE 18 STITCH NEATLY IN THE DITCH ALONG THE SEAM LINE.

MITRING CORNERS

A mitred corner gives a crisp professional look to pockets, borders, trims and hems, reducing some of the bulk of the fabric. It is easier to make a symmetrical mitre if the two seam or hem allowances are more less the same width. If they are very different, a mock mitre might be more appropriate, the instructions for which are on p. 45.

1 Using chalk, mark the fold lines on both of the edges to be mitred.

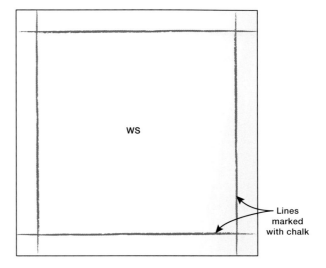

Lines marked with chalk

FIGURE 19 MARK THE FOLD LINES ALONG THE EDGES TO BE MITRED.

2 Fold the corner to the wrong side, folding exactly where the marked lines cross and so the folded fabric makes a triangle with two equal sides. Press the fold.

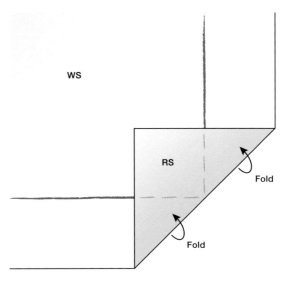

FIGURE 20 FOLD THE CORNER OVER.

3 Unfold the corner and then refold the fabric, right sides together, through the point where the marked lines cross and matching them up along their length. Sew across the seam allowance, starting at the point where the marked lines cross and at right angles to the fold.

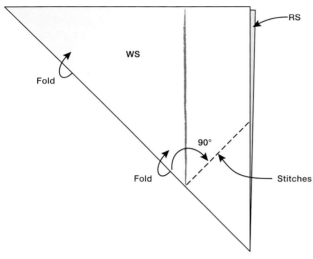

FIGURE 21 SEW ACROSS THE SEAM ALLOW TO MAKE A 90-DEGREE ANGLE WITH THE FOLD.

4 Trim the fabric close to the line of stitching, cutting off the lower triangle. If the fabric frays easily, leave a tiny seam allowance and neaten the raw edge.

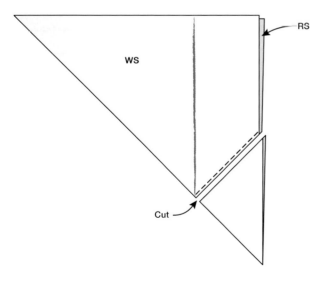

FIGURE 22 TRIM THE EXCESS FABRIC AT THE CORNER TO REDUCE BULK.

5 Press the seam open and then turn the corner out using a point turner.

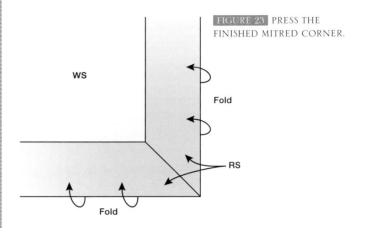

FIGURE 23 PRESS THE FINISHED MITRED CORNER.

PIVOTING AROUND CORNERS

Sew up to the corner, finishing with the needle in the fabric. Lift the foot and pivot the work, lining up the next line for stitching. Lower the foot and continue stitching.

COVERING BUTTONS

1 To make a fabric covered button cut a circle of fabric one and a half times to twice the diameter of the button form.

2 Sew a running stitch around the outer edge of the fabric and place the button form in the centre on the wrong side.

3 Pull up the thread so that the fabric covers the button form and stitch to hold it in place.

4 Push the raw fabric edges into the cavity of the button form and cover with the backing disk.

5 Push the disk into place with the help of pliers, remembering to protect the button front in the process.

ADDING TRIMS

Attaching trims to curtains can cover seam lines, add attractive detail to plain curtains or add a luxurious finishing touch to formal curtains. Trims can be added in the seam, to the reverse of the curtain so just the beading or fringing is visible or to the surface on the right side. The method of application will depend largely on the type of trim; some have plain tapes which are best concealed, other trims have decorative ribbons or tapes which add to the finished look.

ATTACHING TRIM IN A SEAM

1 Place the trim along the curtain edge, right sides together, with the plain tape edge of the trim matching the raw edge of the curtain. Stitch the trim in place down the centre of the tape.

FIGURE 24 ATTACH THE TRIM DOWN THE MIDDLE OF THE TAPE.

2 Place the trimmed fabric on top of the second layer of fabric, right sides together, sandwiching the trim. Using a zipper foot, stitch the seam, sewing as close to the trim as possible. Press.

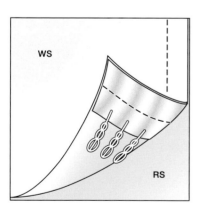

FIGURE 25 USE THE FIRST LINE OF STITCHING AS A GUIDE FOR THE SEAM.

SEWING SENSE

Place the work under the needle with the first stitching holding the tape in place visible so that you can sew easily to the right of the stitching, closer to the actual trim.

3 Turn the fabric to the right side and press. Only the decorative part of the trim will be visible at the seam edge. If desired, top stitch, using a zipper foot to sew close to the edge.

FIGURE 26 TURN THE FABRIC RIGHT SIDE OUT TO ALLOW THE TRIM TO HANG FREELY.

STITCHING TRIM TO THE REVERSE

1 Place the trim along the curtain edge, right sides together, with the plain tape edge of the trim matching the raw edge of the curtain. Stitch the trim in place down the centre of the tape. Press the stitching.

2 Fold the curtain edge to the wrong side so only the trim is visible on the right side. Press and pin in place.

3 Top stitch the hem in place, stitching ³⁄₈in (1cm) from the raw edge.

FIGURE 27 HAVING STITCHED THE TRIM TO THE RIGHT SIDE, TURN THE HEM TO THE WRONG SIDE AND TOP STITCH ³⁄₈IN (ICM) FROM THE EDGE.

STITCHING TRIM TO THE SURFACE

You can stitch trim along an edge or at any distance you want from the edge. You can also stitch trim over the top stitching of a hem or so it drops below the bottom edge of the hem.

1 Decide on the best position for the trim. With chalk, mark a guideline for one edge of the trim to ensure it is straight. Pin the trim in place if you wish.

2 Select a straight or decorative stitch to machine down both long edges of the trim. For some types of trim, such as beading, it may be necessary to use a zipper foot so you can move the needle position as close as possible to the edge of the trim.

RS

FIGURE 28 ATTACH TRIMS WITH STRAIGHT OR DECORATIVE STITCHES.

EXPERT TIP

STITCH ALONG BOTH LONG EDGES OF TRIM IN THE SAME DIRECTION (FROM TOP TO BOTTOM) TO PREVENT IT FROM BUCKLING OR TWISTING.

TRAINING CURTAINS TO HANG WELL

Curtains can be trained to hang in straight, neat folds. You will need 2in-wide (5cm-wide) strips of fabric or paper to wrap around the curtains (these can be joined pieces because they will only be used temporarily).

1 Hang the curtains and open them fully. Starting at the top, guide the pleats into position all the way down the curtain, catching the lining into the folds as you go. Work to about one-third of the way down from the top, holding the pleats together in one hand as you guide the next.

2 When the top third of the curtain is neatly pleated right across its width, tie a strip of fabric or paper around the pleats to hold them in place.

3 Continue down the curtain to neaten the next third, again straightening and folding pleat by pleat. Secure the pleats with fabric or paper.

4 Fold and secure the pleats at the hem line in the same manner.

5 Leave the ties in place for at least 24 hours and preferably for up to a week.

FIGURE 29 FOLD THE PLEATS NEATLY BEFORE BINDING THEM WITH FABRIC OR PAPER STRIPS.

HARDWARE

CURTAINS CAN BE HUNG FROM
RODS, TRACKS, DECORATIVE POLES
OR FIXED BATTENS (WOODEN
FRAMES). THEY ARE ATTACHED BY
HOOKS, RINGS OR CLIPS AND, OF
COURSE, THERE IS A HUGE VARIETY
OF EACH AVAILABLE. HERE IS A
BRIEF EXPLANATION OF THE MOST
COMMON HARDWARE.

Rods

RODS

Rods are usually used for café-style curtains that are attached within the window frame. The curtains have a casing at the top through which the rod is inserted. The rod itself is completely hidden, so it doesn't need to match the décor. The curtain top is then simply gathered along the rod. You can create variations on the basic principle by having deep casings, a standing ruffle above the casing or a self-valance that folds down over the front of the casing.

POLES

Although similar to rods, poles are usually visible and thus decorative. They are usually hung above the window frame and can be made from wood or metal. Available in different sizes, they can be used with curtain rings to hang many types of curtain, with tab-top curtains or with curtains with eyelets, which are threaded onto the pole. Cup hooks are an easy way to hold a pole in place.

FINIALS

These are the decorative features at each end of a pole. They are meant to be on view and extend beyond the top edge of the curtain.

CURTAIN RINGS

These range from big wooden or metal rings, which slide onto decorative poles, to smaller eyelet rings or sew-on rings. Eyelet rings hook through eyelets in the header tape and then slide onto a pole. Sew-on curtain rings are usually sewn onto the back of lightweight curtains, such as café curtains, and slipped onto a concealed pole so they are hidden from view.

Finials

Wooden poles

Metal pole

Eyelets

Finial

TRACKS

Curtain tracks are particularly useful because they bend around curves and bay windows. They are fixed to the wall above the window frame and then hidden by the top of the curtain. Curtain hooks are needed to attach the curtains to the track.

CURTAIN AND VALANCE TRACK

Special attachments for adding a valance overlapping the track are available so that a pair of curtains will overlap when closed. You can also get curtain-pulling mechanisms that allow you to draw the curtain along a pulley at the outside edge or with a thin pole at the leading edge. These are useful for large heavy curtains, those that are difficult to reach or curtains in light or delicately coloured fabric.

HOOKS

Curtain hooks are attached to the header tape at the back of the curtain and then either hooked onto curtain rings or straight onto curtain tracks. There are various shapes of hook to suit the different header tapes, for example, long-necked, four-prong hooks are used with deep pleat header tape, while small curly plastic hooks are used on regular pleated curtains.

CURTAIN CLIPS

There is a wide variety of curtain clips available in many different designs and finishes. They are ideal for hanging lightweight curtains and voiles. You don't need a special header on the curtain, so clips are a very quick and easy solution to curtain toppers. The circular end is slipped onto a curtain rod or attached to a curtain ring and the clip end works like a bulldog clip to hold onto the curtain.

EYELETS

Another simple but decorative finish, eyelets are metal rings to make holes in the top of the curtain. The curtain can then be slipped onto the pole through the eyelets or attached using a decorative cord wound around the pole and through the eyelets. Available in different colours, two-part eyelets are clipped together on the front and back of the curtain, thus hiding the raw edges of the eyelet hole.

WEIGHTS

These are inserted into the hem allowance of curtains to help keep them hanging straight and true. Penny weights look like flat lead buttons and are stitched into the bottom corners of the curtain. Weighting tape looks like a string of slim lead sausages held in a fine net. It comes in different weights and is laid along the bottom fold of the hem before it is stitched in place.

CORD TIDY

Keep the header tape cords tidy by attaching either a toggle or a purpose-made cord tidy approximately 1in (2.5cm) from the side edge. Once the curtain pleats are pulled up to the required width, simply wind the tape around the toggle to keep it from dangling in view or getting tangled.

TIEBACKS

While these can be made from fabric and stiffener to match the curtains, ready-made tiebacks are also available in a wide variety of finishes including beads, feathers or tassels.

Tassle tieback

Weights

Metal curtain clips
Plastic curtain clips

FABRIC

A GOOD CHOICE OF FABRIC CAN MAKE ALL THE DIFFERENCE TO HOW A WINDOW TREATMENT, AND ULTIMATELY YOUR ROOM, WILL LOOK. THERE IS AN ABUNDANCE OF FURNISHING FABRICS AVAILABLE IN DIFFERENT TYPES, WEIGHTS AND PATTERNS. BEFORE MAKING YOUR CHOICE, IT'S IMPORTANT, THEREFORE, TO MAKE SURE YOU CONSIDER WHAT THE FABRIC WILL BE USED FOR, WHETHER THE COLOUR WILL ENHANCE THE REST OF THE DÉCOR AND WHETHER THE TEXTURE OF THE FABRIC AND THE SIZE OF ANY PATTERN WILL WORK WELL IN THE ENVIRONMENT.

Woven fabrics dominate the soft furnishing market. They are woven with warp threads running the length of the fabric and weft (or woof) threads running across the width. They can be plainly woven or have ribbed patterns, twill (diagonal lines on the surface) or a pile or texture giving a velvety surface.

The type of fabric you choose will depend on personal preference and the purpose of the room and the window treatment. You will certainly need to consider:
- the practicalities of the fabric, for example, whether it needs to be hard-wearing, block out sunlight or keep in warmth
- the way the fabric handles and drapes; you may want it to hold pleats crisply, drape softly or puddle on the floor
- the overall effect of the fabric, whether that is a light airy feel or a rich sumptuous look.

Different types of fabric generally suit formal, informal or casual settings. For example, for formal treatments, as in the drawing room, master bedroom, hallway or library, you could use brocade, damask, moiré, silk, velvet or velveteen. In informal settings, such as dining and living rooms, bedrooms and bathrooms, chintz, cotton sateen, linen, seersucker are suitable. More casual window treatments in the kitchen, kitchen/diner or bathroom require serviceable fabrics such as calico, canvas, denim, gingham, muslin, poplin and voile.

For advice on choosing and using patterned fabrics, see pp. 102–105.

CHOOSE A FABRIC OF AN APPROPRIATE WEIGHT AND WITH A SIZE OF PATTERN SUITED TO THE ROOM AND THE SIZE OF THE WINDOW.

CONSIDER HOW THE FABRIC WILL DRAPE. SHOULD IT BE SOFT ENOUGH TO PUDDLE ON THE FLOOR OR CRISP ENOUGH TO HOLD FIRM PLEATS.

LARGE BOLD PATTERNS LOOK GREAT ON BIG WINDOWS.

FABRIC BASICS

It is useful to know several terms associated with fabric.

- The **selvages** run along both edges of the length of the fabric. Manufactured as the weft threads turn, they bind the long edges of the fabric and stop it unravelling.
- The **straight**, or **lengthwise**, **grain** refers to the warp threads that run along the length of the fabric parallel to the selvages. The straight grain is usually the most stable.
- The **crossgrain** runs across the fabric width with the weft threads from selvage to selvage and are thus at right angles to the straight grain.
- The **bias** is a 45-degree diagonal line from one selvage to the other. The true bias is found by folding the cut edge to lie on top of a selvage, laying the crossgrain in the same direction as the straight grain. The fabric will stretch most along the true bias.

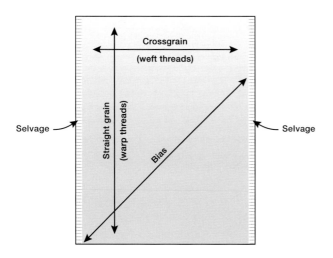

FIGURE 1   FABRIC WILL STRETCH LEAST ALONG THE STRAIGHT GRAIN AND MOST ACROSS THE BIAS.

DEALING WITH SELVAGES

The selvages are usually more tightly bound than the main fabric so it is usually better to cut them off to prevent the curtain puckering or twisting at the edges. However, sometimes you can match a pattern more easily by seaming the two pieces of fabric together just inside the selvage, using it as a seam allowance. In that case, snip into the selvage every 3–4in (7.5–10cm) so the fabric will lie flat.

FIGURE 2   SNIP ACROSS THE SELVAGE TO PREVENT SEAMS PUCKERING AND TWISTING.

FABRIC WIDTHS

Soft furnishing fabrics generally come in two main widths: 45/48in (115/122cm) or 54in (138cm). Occasionally you will find cottons that are 60in (150cm) wide.

The width given on the bolt includes the selvages, which may not be useable. If you do cut them off, remember to recalculate the fabric width by the reduced amount.

FABRIC SHRINKAGE

Many furnishing fabrics should not be washed after being made up into curtains. Some fabrics shrink when washed and others are treated with special finishes, to resist dirt and retain the sheen, which would be destroyed by washing. Therefore, for curtains that will need to be washed, such as those in the kitchen, avoid using treated fabrics. If necessary, have curtains dry-cleaned, although they may still shrink.

EXPERT TIP

VACUUM CURTAINS THOROUGHLY AND REGULARLY. IF POSSIBLE, YOU COULD ALSO TUMBLE THEM IN A TUMBLE DRYER WITH A FEW SHEETS OF FABRIC SOFTENER, WHICH WILL ABSORB THE DIRT.

PATTERN REPEAT

Most furnishing fabrics have a pattern, often repeated down the length of the fabric, either woven in or printed on the front. When making up curtains with more than one width of fabric, you will need to match the pattern across the curtains. See pp. 104–105 for guidance on how to measure the repeat and match the pattern perfectly.

STRAIGHTENING FABRIC

Before marking out and cutting curtain panels, first make sure the cut edge is straight by squaring the fabric. The easiest way is to use a set square.

Place one edge of the square down the edge of the selvage so that the other edge of the square sits across the fabric width. Mark across the fabric width. Hopefully the pattern on the fabric runs parallel to the line.

Mark the new cross grain

FIGURE 3 USE A LARGE SET SQUARE TO MARK A LINE PERPENDICULAR TO THE SELVAGE.

If not, line the set square up with the pattern across the width of the fabric, so that the right angle of the square is close to the edge of the selvage. Mark the lengthwise line close to the selvage. Cut along this line and use this cut edge as the new fabric edge. If the pattern is more than 4cm (1½in) off square, don't use the fabric for curtains, as trying to square it up will waste too much fabric.

FIGURE 4 PLACE THE SET SQUARE ALONG THE HORIZONTAL PATTERN AND THEN MARK THE NEW STRAIGHT GRAIN.

Mark the new straight grain

SEWING SENSE

Mark and cut out fabric on a large flat surface. If using a table or bed, make sure that any excess fabric doesn't hang over the edge, possibly distorting the fabric. Instead, use a chair, ironing board or stool to support the remaining fabric.

CALCULATING HOW MUCH FABRIC TO BUY

The amount of fabric you need is determined by the size of the window, the width of the fabric and the type of header tape. (If your fabric has a pattern, you will also need to take the pattern repeat into account; this is dealt with on pp. 104–105.) Always start by taking accurate window measurements.

THIS WINDOW IS 55IN (140CM) WIDE AND THE FABRIC WAS 54IN (140CM) WIDE. FOR THE CURTAIN TO HAVE DOUBLE FULLNESS, TWO WIDTHS OF FABRIC WERE NEEDED.

MEASURING AROUND WINDOWS

Most curtains, with the exception of café curtains, extend beyond the window frame all around so that when they are open most of the window is visible, letting in maximum light.

FIGURE 5 MEASURE THE LENGTH (DROP) AND THE WIDTH READY TO CALCULATE THE QUANTITY OF FABRIC YOU NEED.

To determine the finished width of the curtains, measure the length of the pole, rail or track. If this has not yet been erected, allow at least 6–8in (15–20cm) on each side of the window frame.

For the finished length (basic drop) of the curtains, decide on how far you want the curtains to fall. That might be to the windowsill, just beyond (apron length), full length (½in (1.25cm) from the floor), to puddle on the floor or any length to suit your needs. Measure from where you want the top of the curtains to sit in relation to the pole, rail or track down to the point where you want the hem of the curtain to rest. If the pole, rail or track has not yet been erected, allow 4–8in (10–20cm) above the window frame.

You could take these basic measurements into your fabric store so that, once you have decided on the fabric and curtain style, the assistant can calculate the total quantity of fabric you need. However, you could make this calculation yourself.

CALCULATING FABRIC QUANTITIES

First you must calculate how many widths of fabric you need and then multiply that by the basic drop, adding allowances for header turnings, hems and the pattern repeat.

LINING QUANTITIES

Calculate the amount of lining needed in the same way as for the main fabric.

CALCULATING HOW MANY WIDTHS ARE NEEDED

The fabric width is used across the curtain and window. To achieve the full width needed for a curtain, you may have to join fabric widths (panels). You may need to join two or more fabric widths, or even cut one fabric width in half and join each half to a single width to get 1½ widths per curtain. This will depend on the window width, the style of the curtains (and therefore the type of header tape), and how full (gathered) they are to be. The nature and properties of the fabric (for example, its weight, stiffness and thickness) will also have a bearing on the amount of fabric you decide to use.

The width of a curtain could be as little as 1½ times the width of the window, so it is not totally flat. However, generally, they are at least twice, if not three times, the window width in fullness.

In making your calculations, you must also factor in the seams and side hems. This will depend on the fabric used, but as a general rule, allow (2–2⅜in (5–6cm) for each seam (i.e. two seam allowances) and 1–1⅛in (2.5–3cm) for each side hem.

Example

For a window of 63in (160cm) wide, you might chose to have twice the window width for fullness. Thus you need 126in (320cm) plus 4–4¾in (10–12cm) for seams and side hems, which, rounded up, gives a total of 131in (332cm). Divide the total width of the curtain by the width of the fabric, for example:

- if the fabric is 45in (114cm) wide, you will need three widths of fabric to achieve the full 131in (332cm)
- if the fabric is 54in (137cm) wide, you will need approx 2½ widths. You will need to buy 3 widths and could perhaps use the excess half width for cushion covers or matching tiebacks.

EXPERT TIP

DON'T WORRY IF THE FULL WIDTH OF FABRIC IS SLIGHTLY DIFFERENT FROM WHAT YOU CALCULATED. YOU CAN MAKE SMALL ADJUSTMENTS BY TAKING MORE OR LESS FABRIC INTO THE SEAMS AND SIDE HEMS, AND ANY EXTRA FULLNESS UNDER 6IN (12CM) CAN BE GATHERED INTO THE HEADER.

SEWING SENSE

When you have to buy more fabric than needed to obtain the total width of the curtain, decide whether to leave the extra width on and just gather more, or whether to cut it off and use the excess fabric to make matching tiebacks or cushion covers.

CALCULATING THE LENGTH NEEDED

The total length of fabric you need to buy is calculated by multiplying the total drop, including allowances for the header turning and the hem, by the number of widths needed. (You may also need to add an allowance for the pattern repeat, which is explained on p. 104.)

Start by adding 8in (20cm), which is suitable for most curtain headers, and 4–8in (10–20cm) for the hem allowance to the basic drop. (Specific allowances for different types of curtain header are given in the projects.) Multiply this figure by the number of widths needed.

Example

- For a drop of 41in (104cm), add 12in (30cm) for header and hems, and 16in (41cm) for the pattern repeat, giving a total length for one panel of 69in (175cm).
- Multiply this length by the number of widths required. If you need three widths, the total length will be 207in (525cm).
- Convert the measurement to yards (metres) and round it up to give 5¾yd (5.25m).

SEWING SENSE

Keep a note of the total drop, including allowances, so that when you are ready to cut out the curtain panels, you have that crucial measurement handy.

CUTTING OUT FABRIC

Lay the fabric on a flat surface such as a table or the floor. If using a table and there is excess fabric, don't allow it to just drape over the edge as this might distort the fabric and pull it out of alignment. Use a chair or smaller table to support the weight of the overhang.

Once each panel is measured and marked, check any pattern match again before cutting. Then use good shears to cut the panels out. See p.105 for advice on cutting half panels.

The Projects

MAKING CASINGS & CONCEALED SEAMS

CASINGS, CHUNNELS OR CHANNELS ARE ALL TERMS TO DESCRIBE A STITCHED TUNNEL THROUGH WHICH THE HARDWARE FOR SUPPORTING THE CURTAIN IS FED. THEY ARE PROBABLY THE EASIEST TYPE OF CURTAIN HEADER TO MAKE AND DON'T REQUIRE ANY SPECIAL EQUIPMENT OR STITCH TECHNIQUE.

CONCEALED SEAMS ARE VERY USEFUL WHEN THE WRONG SIDE OF A CURTAIN WILL BE VISIBLE, FOR EXAMPLE ON UNLINED CAFÉ CURTAINS OR VOILES. THE QUICKEST METHOD IS A FRENCH SEAM, BUT THERE ARE ALSO TWO OTHER GREAT OPTIONS — THE MOCK FRENCH SEAM AND THE FLAT-FELL SEAM.

TOOLS AND EQUIPMENT
✓ Basic sewing kit (see p. 8)

CASING CHOICES

- Make a basic casing, a casing with an upper frill or casing with a pelmet. The instructions for all three variations are given here.

- Consider whether the casing should be made of the same fabric as the curtains or in contrasting fabric.

- Use voile to make curtains with casings or café curtains to let in the maximum light.

SEWING SENSE
Always press a seam before sewing over it again. Failure to do so can result in wrinkles, ridges and unsightly bulk that can't be removed later. Pressing will embed the stitches and flatten the seam.

CALCULATING FABRIC REQUIREMENTS FOR A BASIC CASING

A basic casing consists of a simple stitched tunnel, which is made from the same length of fabric as the main curtain.

Calculate the total amount of fabric you will need as follows. (For more on calculating fabrics, see pp. 30–31; if you need to allow for a fabric repeat, see pp. 104–105.)

1 Decide how many drops you need to make the full width of the curtain, allowing for twice the width for fullness and remembering to add allowances for seams and side hems.

2 Determine the total drop of the main curtain, allowing 4in (10cm) for the hem and an extra allowance for the casing so it slips along the pole, or other support, comfortably. For a basic casing, first measure the circumference of the pole. To this, add at least 1in (2.5cm) for ease and 3/8–1 1/4in (1–3.25cm) for turning under the hem.

Pole circumference + 1in (2.5cm)

3/8–1 1/4in (1–3.25cm)

RS

FIGURE 1 ALLOW ENOUGH FABRIC FOR THE CASING TO GLIDE ALONG THE POLE.

3 Multiply the length of the total drop by the number of drops you need.

MAKING UP A BASIC CASING

1 Sew all the fabric panels for the curtain together (see p. 18 for sewing seams). Neaten the seams and press them to one side. Hem the side edges. Turn up and stitch the bottom hem. Press.

EXPERT TIP

PRESSING THE SEAMS IN THE SAME DIRECTION ALLOWS THE CURTAIN POLE TO RUN MORE SMOOTHLY THROUGH THE CASING.

2 Fold under the casing allowance and tuck the raw edge under again. With the wrong side facing, stitch along the bottom of the casing about 1/4in (6mm) from the turned edge. Measure up from the stitched line the pole diameter plus ease and mark a parallel line. Stitch along this line to form the casing. Press.

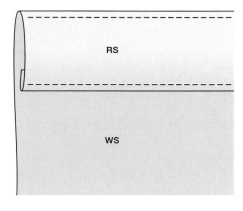

FIGURE 2 STITCH ALONG THE TOP AND BOTTOM FOLDS OF THE CASING.

RS

WS

3 Feed the pole through the casing and gather the curtain evenly across the width.

MAKING A CASING WITH AN UPPER FRILL

This type of casing simply requires more fabric than the basic casing to form a frill along the top edge of the curtain.

1 Calculate the total casing allowance as for the basic casing, but adding to the basic pole circumference: 1in (2.5cm) for ease, 3/8in (1cm) for the turning, plus a further 3in (7.5cm) for the frill.

2 Once the curtain panels have been sewn together and the hem is stitched and pressed, turn under the total casing allowance, including the frill, and tuck the raw edge under.

3 Follow step 2 for making up the basic casing (left). The additional fabric above the casing forms the frill.

FIGURE 3 SEW THE TOP LINE OF STITCHES TO ALLOW FOR THE FRILL ABOVE.

RS

WS

4 Feed the pole through the casing and gather the curtain evenly across the width.

MAKING A CASING WITH A PELMET

This is another variation on the casing style. This time, a much larger amount of fabric is added to the extension so that it folds down over the front of the pole. Follow the steps for the casing with a frill, adding at least 8in (20cm) to the casing allowance. When finished, allow the pelmet to flop over the front of the pole and curtain.

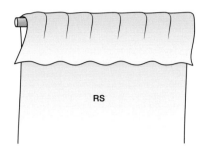

FIGURE 4 ADD AT LEAST 8IN (20CM) TO THE CASING FOR A PELMET.

MAKING A CONTRASTING CASING

Casings can also be made from fabric that contrasts with the main curtain to be showcased as a design feature. The same technique can be adapted to make a concealed casing on the wrong side of the curtain.

1 To calculate the depth of the casing fabric, add to the pole diameter: 1in (2.5cm) for ease, plus 1½in (4cm) for seams.

2 The total width needed will be the same as the curtain width. Join strips as necessary (for example, if the curtain needs three panels, cut three strips of fabric for the casing).

3 If you have more than one strip, join the short ends together, taking ³⁄₈in (1cm) seams. Press the seam allowances to one side, all in the same direction. Hem the short side edges by folding under ³⁄₈in (1cm) and then again. Press. Turn under a ¾in (2cm) hem along the top and bottom of the strip and press.

4 Position the contrast strip on the main curtain, making sure the folded seam line runs parallel to the top of the curtain. Pin and stitch the strip in position along both long edges. Press.

SEWING CONCEALED SEAMS

For unlined curtains, choose a French seam, mock French seam or a flat fell seam, which are ideal for concealing raw edges and giving a neat finish. A flat fell seam is also useful for reducing bulk when two seams, for example on the main curtain and the lining, lie on top of each other. However, none of these seams are suitable for curved seams because you cannot clip across the seam allowance.

FRENCH SEAM

1 With the wrong sides of the fabric together, sew a plain seam ³⁄₈in (1cm) from the edge. Trim the seam allowance to a scant ¼in (6mm). Press the seam to one side. Turn the fabric so that the right sides are facing and the original seam line is on the fold.

FIGURE 5 TURN THE FABRIC SO RIGHT SIDES ARE FACING.

2 Stitch a second seam approximately ³⁄₈in (1cm) from the edge. Open out the fabric and press the seam to one side.

FIGURE 6 STITCH THE SECOND SEAM, ENCLOSING THE FIRST.

MOCK FRENCH SEAM

1 Sew a plain seam with the right sides together, using a seam allowance of ⁵/₈in (1.5cm).

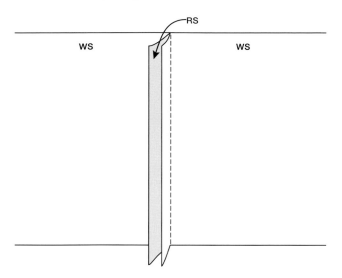

SEW THE FIRST SEAM RIGHT SIDES TOGETHER.

2 On the wrong side, tuck the raw edges of the seam allowance in and pin them together. Stitch close to the folded edges to conceal the raw edges. Press the seam to one side.

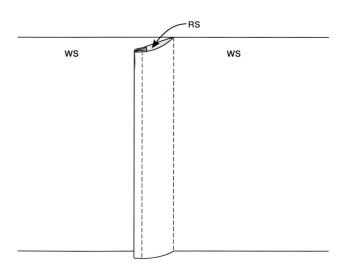

FIGURE 8 STITCH THE SEAM ALLOWANCE EDGES TOGETHER.

SEWING SENSE

Always press seams before trimming the seam allowance.

FLAT FELL SEAM

1 Place the wrong sides of the fabric together and sew a plain seam ⁵/₈in (1.5cm) from the edge. Press both seam allowances, then trim the lower seam allowance to ¹/₈in (3mm).

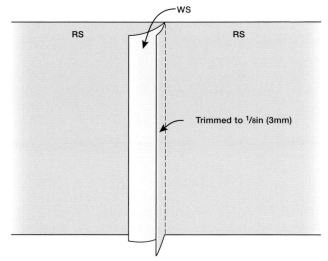

FIGURE 9 SEW THE FIRST SEAM WRONG SIDES TOGETHER.

2 Turn the upper seam allowance edge under and pin it over the trimmed edge. Top stitch, close to the visible fold, through all the layers.

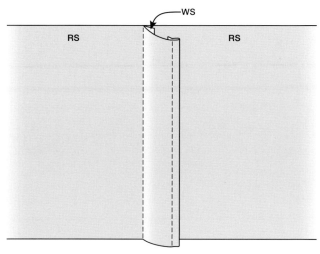

FIGURE 10 FOLD THE WIDER SEAM ALLOWANCE OVER TO CONCEAL THE RAW EDGES.

SEWING SEAMS FOR SHEERS

Instructions for hairline seams and narrow overcast seams, which are particularly suitable for sheer fabrics, are given on p. 81.

cosy CAFÉ CURTAINS

CAFÉ CURTAINS ARE TRADITIONALLY
HUNG ACROSS THE MIDDLE OF THE
WINDOW ON A POLE FED THROUGH A
CASING. THEY PROVIDE AN EASY
SOLUTION TO DRESSING A KITCHEN
WINDOW, GIVING SOME PRIVACY
WHILE STILL ALLOWING IN SOME
NATURAL LIGHT. BECAUSE THEY ARE
NOT LINED, FRENCH SEAMS ARE IDEAL
FOR FINISHING THE BACK OF CAFÉ
CURTAINS NEATLY.

FABRIC CALCULATION

1 Measure the basic curtain drop from the pole to the windowsill.
Then add:
- 8in (20cm) for the casing and upper frill
- 4in (10cm) for the hem.

2 For the width, measure the length of the pole. Then:
- double the measurement for fullness
- add an allowance for seams and side hems (see p. 30).
  If you prefer to keep things simple, you can just add an allowance of 4in (10cm) for all the seams and side hems in this project.

3 Work out how many widths of fabric you need. Then multiply the total drop by the number of widths to give you the total length of fabric (see pp. 30–31).

YOU WILL NEED

✓ Lightweight fabric (as calculated above)
✓ 1 reel of general-purpose sewing thread
✓ Basic sewing kit (see p. 8)
✓ Pole or dowelling
✓ 2 cup hooks

TECHNICAL KNOW-HOW

Calculating fabric requirements (see pp. 30–31)
Sewing a French seam (see p. 36)
Making casings (see pp. 35–36)

MAKING THE CURTAINS

1 With the right side uppermost, cut the first panel of fabric, including the allowances. Cut the remaining panels, matching any pattern as necessary (see pp. 104–105). Trim away the selvages on each panel (see p. 28).

2 Pin and sew the panels together, using French seams to conceal the raw edges and keep the wrong side of the curtain looking neat (see p. 36). Press the seam allowances to one side, in the same direction.

3 Turn under the raw edges by ³⁄₈in (1cm) once, and then again to make a double hem down each side edge. Stitch the side hems and press.

4 Turn a 4in (10cm) double hem along the bottom edge of the curtain, turning under 2in (5cm) once, and then again. Machine the hem in place close to the top folded edge. Press.

SEWING SENSE
Sew the hem in place by hand for an invisible finish on the right side.

MAKING THE CASING

1 To make the top frill and casing for the pole, with the wrong side uppermost, fold the raw edge of the curtain under by 8in (20cm) and press. Tuck a ³⁄₈in (1cm) hem under and pin through all the layers.

2 Recheck the measurement from the top of the pole to the windowsill to ensure that the pinned line will be at least 1in (2.5cm) below the pole. Adjust the depth of the casing if necessary. Then machine stitch along the line of pins, removing them in the process.

3 Machine another line of stitches above the first line, allowing at least ½in (1.25cm) in addition to the pole diameter, to form the casing (see p. 35). Press.

4 Feed the pole through the casing, adjust the gathers and hang the curtain at the window.

EXPERT TIP
CAFÉ CURTAINS LOOK LOVELY IN VOILE, WHICH GIVES YOU SOME PRIVACY WHILE LETTING IN LOTS OF LIGHT. SEE PP. 80—81 FOR GUIDANCE ON SEWING WITH SHEERS.

MAKING TAB-TOP CURTAINS

TAB-TOP CURTAINS ARE EASY TO MAKE AND DON'T REQUIRE ANY SPECIALIST HEADER TAPES. THE TABS HANG OVER THE CURTAIN POLE AND ALLOW THE CURTAIN TO BE DRAWN FREELY ALONG IT. THE METHOD DESCRIBED HERE IS SUITABLE FOR SIMPLE RECTANGLES OR SHAPES THAT CAN BE TOP-STITCHED IN PLACE OR BUTTONED TO MAKE FLAPS. THE TABS CAN BE LEFT CLASSICALLY PLAIN, MADE FROM CONTRASTING FABRIC OR DRESSED UP WITH BUTTONS OR A VARIETY OF TRIMS.

THIS CHAPTER ALSO EXPLAINS HOW TO FOLD A NEAT MOCK MITRE ON THE BOTTOM CORNERS OF A CURTAIN HEM.

TOOLS AND EQUIPMENT

✓ Basic sewing kit (see p. 8)
✓ Fusible interfacing

TAB-TOP CHOICES

- Basic rectangular tab tops are easy to make, but also consider different shaped tabs such as triangles (explained on pp. 46–50) or tabs with wavy edges.
- You could also adapt the method here to attach two long ties in place of every tab, which can be knotted over the top of the pole and left to hang free.
- Consider using tab-top curtains in a child's bedroom. You could line them with a contrast print and reverse them to change the look whenever you like.

CALCULATING FABRIC REQUIREMENTS

Tab-top curtains cannot be pulled back fully because the tabs sit side by side on the pole. A very full curtain with lots of tabs would therefore be a problem. To avoid that, tab-top curtains are often only 1½ times the window width and certainly no more than twice the width. For example, if a window is 60in (1.5m) wide, the total width of the curtains needs to be between 90in (2.25m) and 120in (3m).

FIGURE 1 A FULLNESS OF 1½–2 TIMES THE WINDOW WIDTH IS SUITABLE FOR TAB-TOP CURTAINS.

Calculate the total amount of fabric you will need as follows.
1 Determine the total drop of the main curtain, allowing 4in (10cm) for the hem and 4in (10cm) for the top turning, remembering to add an amount for seams and side hems (see pp. 30–31). Then decide how many drops you need to make the full width of the curtain.

2 Multiply the length of the total drop by the number of drops you need.

EXPERT TIP
FOR MORE ON CALCULATING FABRICS, SEE P. 30—31;
IF YOU NEED TO ALLOW FOR A FABRIC REPEAT, SEE
PP. 104—105.

3 Add a suitable amount of fabric for the type and number of tabs required. As tabs are usually 2–3in (5–7.5 cm) wide and up to 15in (38 cm) long, allow at least ¼yd (0.25m) for a one-panel curtain. For wider curtains, add a further ¼yd (0.25m) for each drop. However, for finer measurements, take the following points into consideration.

CALCULATING THE FABRIC FOR EACH TAB

4 The width of the tab depends on the weight of the fabric. A lightweight fabric can be supported from narrower tabs, for example 2in (5cm) wide. However sturdier tabs of about 3in (7.5cm) wide are more suitable to take the weight of a heavyweight fabric. Shaped tabs such as the triangular ones on pp. 46–51 may be even wider. Add ¾in (2cm) to the width at the widest part of the tab to allow for the two side seams.

5 The length of the tab is partly determined by the circumference of the pole. Tabs are attached to the front and back of the curtain 1–2in (2.5–5cm) from the top. To calculate the length of fabric for each tab, add to the pole circucmference: 4in (10cm) for attaching the tab to the curtain, 1in (2.5cm) for turning under the ends and 3–5in (7.5–13cm) for a gap between the curtain top and the pole.

Pole circumference 5in (13cm)

Tab width

Tab length

Gap 1½–2½in (4–6.25cm)

1–2in (2.5–5cm)

MEASURE THE DIMENSIONS OF ONE TAB TO HELP CALCULATE THE TOTAL FABRIC REQUIREMENT.

EXPERT TIP
REMEMBER THAT TABS SHOULD BE CUT FROM THE
FABRIC WITH THE LENGTH RUNNING IN THE SAME
DIRECTION AS THE MAIN CURTAIN, ESPECIALLY IF THE
FABRIC HAS A PATTERN.

CALCULATING THE NUMBER OF TABS

6 One tab is positioned close to each top corner of the curtain and the rest are spaced evenly along the top edge of the curtain. The number of tabs is determined by the width of the tabs and the space in between. The space between tabs should be approximately 8in (20cm), although they need to be closer together for heavier curtains than for lightweight ones. The space between the tabs determines how far the curtain can be pulled back to show the window.

Width   Gap

DECIDE ON THE WIDTH OF THE TABS AND THE GAPS TO HELP CALCULATE THE NUMBER OF TABS YOU NEED.

7 Add the width of the tab to the width of the gap. Divide the curtain width by the resulting measurement to calculate the number of tabs.

MAKING A CURTAIN WITH RECTANGULAR TABS

1 Sew all the fabric panels for the curtain together. Neaten the seams and press. Hem the side edges and press. Turn up and stitch the bottom hem. Press.

PREPARING THE CURTAIN FOR A TAB TOP

2 With the wrong side of the curtain uppermost, measure the required drop from the bottom hem to the top, marking across the width. Fold the top down at the marked line and press. Unfold the top and, allowing 4in (10cm) for the turning, trim away any excess fabric.

3 Apply interfacing to the turning allowance on the wrong side of the curtain above the marked line.

FIGURE 4   IRON FUSIBLE INTERFACING TO THE WRONG SIDE OF THE TURNING ALLOWANCE.

4 Turn the raw edge under and top stitch it in place. Fold the turning allowance to the wrong side of the curtain along the marked line and press. Top stitch it in place close to the top fold.

FIGURE 5   STITCH THE TOP EDGE CLOSE TO THE FOLD.

PREPARING THE TABS

5 Cut out the required number of tabs. You need two pieces of fabric and one piece of interfacing for each tab, including seam and turning allowances all around the fabric.

6 Apply interfacing to the wrong side of one piece of fabric for each tab.

7 With right sides facing, sew ⅜in (1cm) seams down the long sides of each tab. Press. Turn the tabs right sides out and press flat. Turn under both ends of the tabs by ½in (13mm).

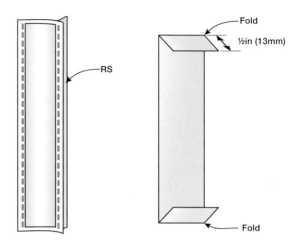

FIGURE 6   PREPARE THE TABS SO THEY ARE ALL PRECISELY THE SAME DIMENSIONS.

ATTACHING THE TABS

8 Pin one end of each tab to the wrong side of the curtain 1–2in (2.5–5cm) from the top.

9 Fold each tab over the top of the curtain and pin it to the right side exactly on top of the other end. Make sure all the tabs are pinned the same distance from the top of the curtain.

10 Attach each tab, by stitching a rectangle though all thicknesses at the base of the tab, effectively stitching the tab ends closed at the same time (NB. Increase the stitch length to accomodate for the thickness of the layers.)

FIGURE 7   SECURE THE TAB BY STITCHING A RECTANGLE CLOSE TO THE EDGES OF THE TAB AND 1IN (2.5CM) DEEP.

11 Leave the tabs plain or finish them with buttons or other applied decoration.

MAKING A MOCK MITRE

When both hems are the same width, a symmetrical mitre is possible (see p. 20–21). However, as most bottom hems are wider than side hems, a mock mitre is often more practical.

1 Turn the bottom hem of the curtain up to make a double hem. Press the hem.

2 Open out the bottom hem and one fold of the unstitched part of the side hem (leave 9in/23cm from the bottom edge unstitched). Lay the side turning flat. Insert a pin into the side turning to mark the bottom edge of the bottom hem. Snip across the side turning 1¾in (4.5cm) above the bottom edge. Tuck the rest of the side turning back under.

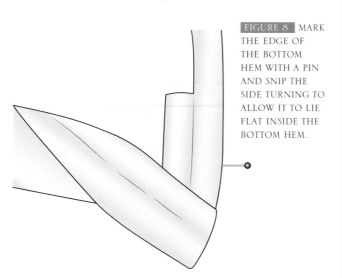

FIGURE 8 MARK THE EDGE OF THE BOTTOM HEM WITH A PIN AND SNIP THE SIDE TURNING TO ALLOW IT TO LIE FLAT INSIDE THE BOTTOM HEM.

3 Refold the bottom hem and, with a pin, mark the width of the side hem on the bottom hem.

FIGURE 9 MARK THE WIDTH OF THE SIDE HEM ON THE BOTTOM HEM.

4 Fold under the side edge of the bottom hem in a diagonal line from the bottom pin to the top pin. Tuck in the excess fabric as neatly as possible.

FIGURE 10 FOLD THE HEM ALLOWANCE TO MAKE A MOCK MITRE.

5 Pin the mitred corner in place and then mitre the other corner. Stitch the mitres in place with slip stitch. Then stitch the rest of the hem by hand, using a lock stitch (see p. 16) or choosing an alternative stitch from p. 15).

FIGURE 11 SLIP STITCH THE MITRE IN PLACE.

SEWING SENSE
If the fabric is bulky or heavyweight trim away excess fabric from the diagonally folded hem allowance, leaving just ¼in (6mm) for a seam allowance.

triangular
TAB-TOP CURTAINS

THE TRIANGULAR TAB TOPS ON THESE
CURTAINS ARE FUN AND WILL LOOK
FABULOUS ON A PRETTY POLE.
HOWEVER, THEY ARE QUICK AND
SIMPLE TO MAKE. BECAUSE THE TABS
ARE TRIANGULAR, THEY ARE
INCORPORATED INTO A SEAM ALONG
THE TOP OF THE CURTAIN. THE
COVERED BUTTONS ADD THE FINAL
DESIGNER DETAIL.

FABRIC CALCULATION

1 Calculate the amount of fabric you need for the basic curtains by measuring the total drop of the curtain, including 4in (10cm) for the hem but only ⅝in (1.5cm) for the top turning. If the fabric has a pattern, you will also need to include the pattern repeat in your calculations (see pp. 104–105). Decide on how many drops you need to make the free width of the curtain, remembering to add an amount for seams and side hems. Multiply the total drop by the number of drops.

2 Calculate an additional amount for a 5in (13cm) deep strip of fabric to finish the top edge, based on the width of the finished curtain, plus side seams.

3 Calculate the additional amount you need for the triangular tabs. Allow about ¼yd for each curtain drop (this should allow 7 x 8in/18 x 20cm for each tab, taking any pattern into account).

EXPERT TIP
MATCH ANY PATTERN ACROSS ALL THE TABS.

YOU WILL NEED

✓ Curtain fabric (as calculated above)
✓ Approximately 2¼yd (2m) of medium-weight fusible interfacing for tabs and 3in (7.5cm strip) across top edge of curtain
✓ Paper and pencil
✓ 2–3 reels of matching thread
✓ ¾in- (2cm-) diameter self-cover button forms for each tab
✓ Basic sewing kit (see p. 8)

TECHNICAL KNOW-HOW

Calculating fabric requirements (see pp. 30–31)
Working with patterned fabric (see pp. 104–105)
Making a mock mitre (see p. 45)
Making tab tops (see pp. 42–44)
Covering buttons (see p. 21)

MAKING THE TAB PATTERN

1 Make a paper pattern for the triangular tabs. Draw a 5½in (14cm) line for the 'base' of the triangle. Mark the centre point and draw a vertical line 6½in (16.5cm) long from the marked point. Join both ends of the first line to the bottom end of the vertical line to form a triangle. This is the finished size of the tab and the outline represents the seam lines.

2 Add a ³⁄₈in (1cm) seam allowance all around the shape. Mark the position for the button, which is 2in (5cm) directly above the finished point of the triangle. Copy the other instructions from the diagram below to complete your paper pattern.

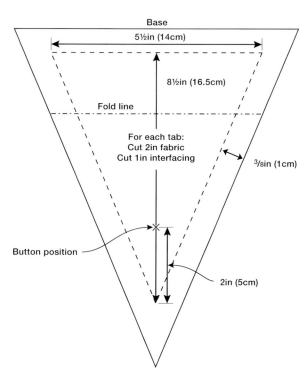

FIGURE 1   TRANSFER THE INSTRUCTIONS ON THE DIAGRAM TO YOUR PAPER PATTERN.

CUTTING OUT

1 With the right side uppermost, cut the first panel of curtain fabric, including the hem and top turning allowances but not the pattern repeat. Cut the remaining panels, matching the pattern as necessary (see pp. 104–105).

2 Cut an additional strip of curtain fabric for each curtain, the same width as the curtain and 5in (13cm) deep.

EXPERT TIP

IF YOU PUT THE CURTAIN PANELS TO ONE SIDE FOR ANY LENGTH OF TIME, FOLD THE FABRIC LENGTHWAYS SO THAT ANY RESULTING STUBBORN CREASES WILL BE DISGUISED WITHIN THE FOLDS OF THE CURTAIN WHEN IT IS HUNG.

3 Cut out two triangular shapes for each tab, using your paper pattern. Cut the front piece for each tab with any pattern running down from the base to the tip of the triangle. Cut the reverse sides with the pattern running from tip to base so that the pattern is the right way up when it is hanging on the pole. Remember to match any pattern across the tabs. Cut one piece of interfacing for each tab.

MAKING THE CURTAINS

1 Pin the curtain fabric panels together, matching any pattern, to make the total width for each curtain. Sew any seams, using straight seams and machine sewing from the hem to the top. Neaten the seam allowances with overcast or zigzag stitch (see p. 18). Press the seams.

2 Turn under the raw edges by 1in (2.5cm) once, and then again to make a double hem down each side edge. Stitch in place, starting 9in (23cm) from the bottom of the curtain. Press.

3 Turn up the bottom hem allowance to make a double hem of 4in (10cm). Press. Make a mock mitre at each end of the hem, following steps 2–5 on p. 45. Stitch the bottom and the rest of the side hems in place. Press.

MAKING AND ATTACHING THE TABS

1 Apply fusible interfacing to the wrong side of the tab fronts. Place the back and the front pieces right sides together. Stitch along the two long sides of each tab, taking two stitches across the sharp point. Trim the stitched edges to ¼in (6mm) and across the point to reduce bulk. Turn the tabs right sides out and press flat.

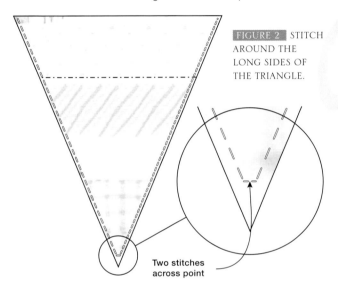

FIGURE 2 STITCH AROUND THE LONG SIDES OF THE TRIANGLE.

Two stitches across point

2 Allowing for a ⅝in (1.5cm) seam along the top edge of the curtain, check the drop. Trim the top edge if necessary. Apply a 3in (7.5cm) strip of fusible interfacing to the wrong side of the curtain just below the seam allowance.

3 Pin the unstitched edge of each tab to the top edge of the curtain, right sides facing and raw edges matching. Position the bottom edge of each end tab at each side edge of the curtain and leave 4in (10cm) gaps between the others.

FIGURE 3 PIN THE TABS IN PLACE.

Raw edges

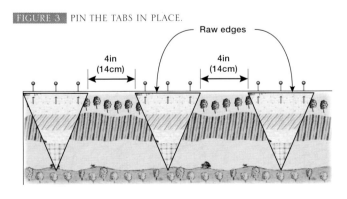

4in (14cm)   4in (14cm)

4 Piece together the fabric strip for the top turning as necessary. Turn and stitch a double hem along one long edge. Press. Along the raw edge, mark the centre of the strip and the curtain. Match the marks and place the strip over the curtain panel, right sides facing and top raw edges matching, sandwiching the tabs between the layers. Pin the strip in place from the centre outwards, so the ends of the strip extend beyond curtain. Sew the strip in place, securing the triangles.

WS

RS   FIGURE 4 PIN THE STRIP IN PLACE FROM THE CENTRE POINT OUTWARDS.

5 Trim the seam allowances along the top edge. Then fold the strip to the wrong side of the curtain and press. Fold in the ends of the strip and pin them in place. Top stitch across the ends of the strip and then across the top edge of the curtain.

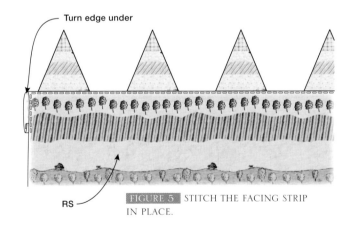

Turn edge under

RS   FIGURE 5 STITCH THE FACING STRIP IN PLACE.

6 Fold the tabs down into position and pin 2in (5cm) above the points. Check the curtain pole slips easily through the tabs. Adjust the pins if necessary and remove the pole.

7 Cover the self-cover button forms with fabric, following the manufacturer's instructions, or see p. 21. Attach a button in place of each pin, sewing through all the layers with a double thread. Slip the pole back through the tabs and hang the curtains.

MAKING TIEBACKS

TIEBACKS HOLD OPEN CURTAINS
BACK FROM THE WINDOW TO LET IN
MORE LIGHT. THEY CAN COORDINATE
WITH THE CURTAINS AND SIMPLY
PERFORM THEIR BASIC FUNCTION, OR
THEY CAN BE A REAL FOCAL POINT.
ALTHOUGH THERE ARE MANY READY-
MADE TIEBACKS AVAILABLE, MAKING
YOUR OWN ENSURES THAT THEY
MATCH YOUR CURTAINS.

METHODS FOR MAKING TWO
DIFFERENT SHAPES OF TIEBACK AND
FOR ADDING PIPING ARE GIVEN IN
THIS CHAPTER.

TOOLS AND EQUIPMENT

✓ Fusible heavyweight interfacing

✓ 2 curtain rings for each tieback

✓ 1 metal cup hook for each tieback

✓ Piping cord, size to suit the size of the
tieback and weight of the fabric

✓ Basic sewing kit (see p. 8)

TIEBACK CHOICES

- You can use ready-made tiebacks of various types,
  including highly decorative tassels.
- Traditional matching tiebacks are made from the same
  fabric as the curtains, often in a crescent shape and
  with piped edges. They are quite rigid, stiffened by a
  heavyweight interfacing (see pp. 54–55), or
  ready-made buckram tieback shapes, as in the
  following project (see p. 61).
- Think about the proportions of the tiebacks. They
  are generally 3–6in (7.5–15cm) wide. Lightweight
  curtains look best with a light narrower tieback, while
  heavyweight curtains look more dramatic with a deeper
  shaped tieback.
- Consider adding scallop shaping to the bottom edge of
  your tiebacks or adding an in-seam trim all around.

DECIDING ON THE SIZE OF TIEBACKS

There are some basic principles
you can follow for creating
tiebacks of pleasing proportions.

← Tape measure

FIGURE 1 MEASURE AROUND
THE FOLDED BACK CURTAIN TO
DECIDE ON THE MOST PLEASING
LENGTH FOR THE TIEBACKS.

1 Pull back the curtain and wrap a tape measure around the folded fabric. Angle the tape measure down towards the leading edge of the curtain. If possible, ask someone else to hold the curtain in position so you can step back and check you are happy with the effect. Take a note of the length of tape used, which gives you the length of the finished tieback.

EXPERT TIP

HANG TIEBACKS FOLLOWING THE 'THIRDS' PRINCIPLE. PLACE THEM TWO-THIRDS DOWN FROM THE TOP OF THE CURTAIN FOR THE MOST PLEASING DRAPE.

2 Also consider how deep you want the tiebacks to be. The heavier the curtain fabric, the deeper the tieback should be so the whole window treatment is well balanced.

EXPERT TIP

HANG THE CURTAINS FIRST AND THEN DECIDE ON THE STYLE OF TIEBACK.

MAKING SIMPLE RECTANGULAR TIEBACKS

The basic method for making tiebacks is easy to master.

1 For each tieback, cut two strips of fabric the length by the width of the finished tieback plus 1in (2.5cm) all around for seams. Alternatively, you could cut the reverse side of the tieback from lining fabric. Cut one piece of interfacing the same size. Apply the interfacing to the wrong side of one piece of fabric.

Length + 1in (2.5cm)

Width + 1in (2.5cm)

FIGURE 2 ADD A SEAM ALLOWANCE ALL AROUND THE BASIC DIMENSIONS.

SEWING SENSE

If using fusible interfacing, trim it to sit just within the seam line before applying it.

2 Stitch the two pieces of fabric right sides together, taking a ½in (1.25cm) seam allowance and leaving an opening along the bottom edge for turning through. Trim the seam allowance across the corners.

WS

FIGURE 3 STITCH AROUND THE TIEBACK, LEAVING AN OPENING FOR TURNING THROUGH.

3 Turn the tieback right sides out. Press, tucking inside the seam allowance across the opening.

4 Slip stitch the opening closed (see p. 15). Attach two curtain rings to the wrong side of the tieback, one on an upper corner, the second at the other end centrally and ¾in (2cm) from the end. Reverse the positioning of the rings on the other tieback.

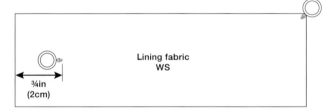

Lining fabric
WS

¾in
(2cm)

FIGURE 4 ATTACH THE TWO RINGS SO THEY WILL BE HIDDEN WHEN HANGING ON THE HOOK.

5 You will need a cup hook fixing in the wall for each tieback. The hook should be at the correct height for the tieback and in line with the outside bracket on the curtain pole. Hang the tieback from the corner curtain ring with the reverse side facing. Take the tieback around the curtain and hang the other ring on the hook, hiding the hardware.

EXPERT TIP

FOR HEAVYWEIGHT CURTAINS, ATTACH TWO CUP HOOKS TO THE WALL ABOUT 2IN (5CM) APART, ONE ON THE WINDOW FRAME AND THE OTHER ON THE WALL IN LINE WITH THE BRACKET ON THE CURTAIN POLE. HOOK THE UNDERSIDE OF THE TIEBACK ON THE FRAME AND THE FRONT SIDE ON THE WALL.

MAKING SHAPED TIEBACKS

You can make tiebacks in different shapes by first making a paper pattern. Here a classic curved shape is described.

1 Make a paper pattern. Draw a rectangle that is the desired width of the tieback by half the desired length. Mark the centre points, top and bottom, along the length. Label the fold line at one end. At the other end, measure 1½–2½in (4–6.5cm) up from each corner. Join the two new corner points with a straight line. Draw a curved line from each new corner to the corresponding centre mark, smoothing the join and making sure the two curves are parallel.

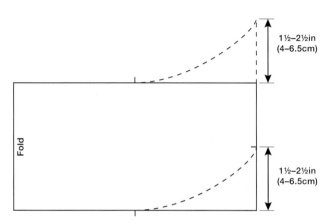

FIGURE 5 CREATE TWO PARALLEL CURVES WITH CAREFUL MEASURING.

2 Add ½in (1.25cm) seam allowance all around, except on the fold line. Cut out the paper pattern. Place the fold line on the fold of the fabric and use the pattern to cut two pieces of fabric and one piece of interfacing for each tieback.

3 Make the tieback in the same manner as for the simple rectangular tieback.

SEWING SENSE

Use either two pieces of the same fabric or one piece of main fabric and one piece of lining fabric to make your tiebacks.

MAKING PIPED TIEBACKS

Piping is a raised rounded trim that gives a crisp finish. You can make it in matching or contrasting fabric. Ready-made piping or flange cord is also available and can be applied in exactly the same way.

1 Cut enough bias strips of fabric 1½in (4cm) wide to go all around the edge of the tieback, plus 3in (7.5cm) extra. To get the full length needed, join the strips on the bias as necessary. Trim the seams and press flat.

FIGURE 6 JOIN BIAS STRIPS AT A 45-DEGREE ANGLE.

2 Fold the bias strip in half lengthways, with wrong sides together, with the piping cord sandwiched in the fold. Using a zipper foot, machine stitch the long edge to hold the piping cord in place.

FIGURE 7 ENCASE THE CORD IN FABRIC TO MAKE THE PIPING.

3 Pin the piping to the right side of the interfaced piece of main fabric, aligning the raw edges and clipping into the seam allowance on the piping so it bends smoothly around the curves and corners. Where the ends of the piping meet, cut the cord 1in (2.5cm) shorter at one end and tuck the piping fabric end under. Lay the other end over the neatened end so that the cord ends meet.

FIGURE 8. JOIN THE CORD AND PIPING FABRIC NEATLY.

SEWING SENSE

Make sure the piping meets along the bottom edge of the tieback.

4 Using the zipper foot, machine stitch the piping in place over the previous stitching.

5 Place the second layer of fabric over the trimmed fabric, right sides together and sandwiching the piping. Using the zipper foot, stitch the seam as close to the piping cord as possible by moving the needle to the left. Leave an opening for turning.

FIGURE 9. SMAKE SURE YOU STITCH THE SEAM LINE CLOSER TO THE PIPING THAN THE PREVIOUS STITCHING.

SEWING SENSE

Work with the piped section uppermost so you can see the previous stitching.

6 Clip into the seam allowances of the fabric and piping tape and press. Turn the tieback to the right side and press again. Finish the tieback in the same way as for the simple rectangular tieback.

A CRESCENT-SHAPED TIEBACK HOLDS CURTAINS BACK BEAUTIFULLY.

beautiful BORDERED CURTAINS

MUCH-LOVED CURTAINS DON'T NEED TO BE DITCHED IF YOU MOVE HOUSE OR TRANSFER THEM TO A BIGGER WINDOW — SIMPLY ENLARGE THEM BY ADDING BORDERS. THESE ZINGY-LOOKING CURTAINS HAVE CONTRASTING BORDERS OF PLAIN FABRIC ON THE OUTER AND BOTTOM EDGES. THEY ALSO INTRODUCE THE USE OF ONE OF THE MOST POPULAR HEADER TAPES — PENCIL PLEAT TAPE.

THE CURTAINS ARE COMPLEMENTED BY PRETTY TIEBACKS MADE FROM BORDER FABRIC AND PIPED WITH THE ORIGINAL CURTAIN FABRIC (SEE P. 60). ALTHOUGH TIEBACKS CAN BE MADE WITH HEAVYWEIGHT INTERFACING, HERE READY-MADE BUCKRAM SHAPES HAVE BEEN USED TO GIVE A REALLY CRISP FINISH. THE BUCKRUM IS TOO STIFF TO SEW THROUGH, SO IT IS HELD IN PLACE WITH INTERFACING AND THE TIEBACKS ARE FINISHED WITH A HAND-SEWN LINING.

FABRIC CALCULATION

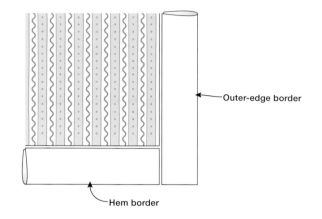

Outer-edge border

Hem border

FIGURE 1 IF POSSIBLE, ADD A DEEPER BORDER ACROSS THE BOTTOM OF THE CURTAIN. ATTACH THE NEW OUTER-EDGE BORDER TO THE EXISTING CURTAIN AND THE BOTTOM BORDER.

1 Calculate the new total drop required (see pp. 30–31).

2 Calculate the new width of curtaining required (see pp. 30–31). Then multiply the measurement by 2½ for fullness. Divide that measurement in half to give the width of fabric needed in each new curtain.

YOU WILL NEED

✓ Pair of curtains to extend
✓ Contrasting fabric for borders (see step 4 p. 58)
✓ Contrasting fabric for tiebacks
✓ Pencil pleat header tape (the total width of the curtains plus 2½in (6.5cm))
✓ 2–3 reels of matching thread
✓ Pair of ready-made buckram tieback shapes
✓ Fusible interfacing
✓ Piping cord
✓ 4 curtain rings
✓ Basic sewing kit (see p. 8)

TECHNICAL KNOW-HOW

Making tiebacks (see pp. 52–55)
Making piping (see pp. 54–55)

3 Remove the header tape and undo the hems on the original curtains. Press the fabric and trim off any obvious creases that will not smooth out, making sure the panels are the same size. Measure the length and width of one curtain.

SEWING SENSE

Save any off-cuts that can be made up into piping for the tiebacks.

4 To calculate the dimensions of one bottom border, which will be self-faced:
• subtract the length of the existing curtains from the new drop required
• double the resulting measurement and add ¾in (2cm) for two seam allowances to give the length of the fabric.
The width of this border is the same as the width of one existing curtain.

5 To calculate the width of one vertical border, which will be self-faced:
• subtract the width of one original curtain from the width of fabric needed for one new curtain
• double the resulting measurement and add ¾in (2cm) for two seam allowances.
The length of the border is the same as the length of the existing curtain, plus the depth of the new bottom border, plus ⅝in (1.5cm) for the bottom seam.

SEWING SENSE

If you use plain fabric for the borders, you can cut them very economically. You may be able to cut matching tiebacks from the off-cuts.

ATTACHING THE BOTTOM BORDERS

1 Cut out two new bottom borders and two new vertical borders. Fold each border in half lengthwise with the wrong sides facing and press.

2 Unfold one bottom border and place it right sides together with the lower edge of the existing curtain. Pin and sew together, taking a ⅜in (1cm) seam allowance and using a straight seam. Press the seam flat, then press the seam allowances towards the border.

FIGURE 2 PRESS THE SEAM ALLOWANCES DOWNWARDS.

3 Turn the remaining long edge of the border over by ⅜in (1cm) and press. Refold the border to the wrong side of the curtain, enclosing the seam allowances. Either slip stitch the border in place or 'stitch in the ditch' (see p. 19), working from the right side and stitching along the previous seam line.

'Stitching in the ditch'

Main fabric RS

Bottom border RS

FIGURE 3 STITCH THE BORDER IN PLACE 'IN THE DITCH'.

4 On the leading edge, fold 1in (2.5cm) and 1in (2.5in) again to make a double side hem down the length of the curtain and border. Pin it in place. At the bottom corner fold up the side hem diagonally to make a mock mitre. Hand stitch the mitre and machine stitch the rest of the hem in place. Press.

FIGURE 4 MITRE THE BOTTOM CORNER OF THE LEADING SIDE HEM.

5 Repeat this method to attach another border along the bottom edge of the other curtain.

ATTACHING THE NEW OUTER-EDGE BORDERS

1 Sew the new border and the curtain together in the same way as for the bottom borders. Position the new border so that the raw edges at the top of the curtain match and the bottom of the border extends beyond the bottom of the curtain.

FIGURE 5 ATTACH THE NEW BORDER TO THE OUTER EDGE OF THE CURTAIN.

2 Press the seam flat, then press the seam allowances towards the border.

3 Fold up a ⅝in (1.5cm) hem on the border and press. Turn the remaining long edge of the border over by ⅜in (1cm) and press. Refold the border, enclosing the seam allowances. Either slip stitch the border in place or 'stitch in the ditch'. Finish the hem edge invisibly with slip stitch. Press.

4 Attach a new border to the other curtain in the same way.

ATTACHING THE HEADER TAPE

1 Lay the curtain on a flat surface and smooth out. Measure the required drop from the bottom edge towards the upper edge and mark with a row of pins or chalk. Fold the excess fabric at the top to the wrong side.

2 Pin the top edge of the header tape in place a scant ¼in (6mm) down from the top of the curtain. Pin the other long edge in the same way, without trimming the ends. On the leading edge machine stitch through the tape only to secure the cords at that end. Trim the tape to about 1¼in (3cm) beyond the width of the curtain and then tuck the raw ends under so that the tape comes to about ¼in (6mm) from the edge of the fabric. Pin the ends.

> ### SEWING SENSE
> *Place the pins on the header tape two finger widths from the end, so you can machine stitch without moving or hitting the pins.*

3 Using the machine, straight stitch the tape in place close to the edges. Start at the bottom left corner, continuing up the side, along the top edge and down the opposite side to the bottom right, keeping the cords out of the way. Secure and cut the threads. Starting again at the bottom left, machine along the bottom of the tape.

FIGURE 6 MACHINE ALONG THE TOP AND BOTTOM OF THE HEADER TAPE IN THE SAME DIRECTION TO STOP IT TWISTING.

4 Pull up the cords in the header tape by the required amount and tie them neatly.

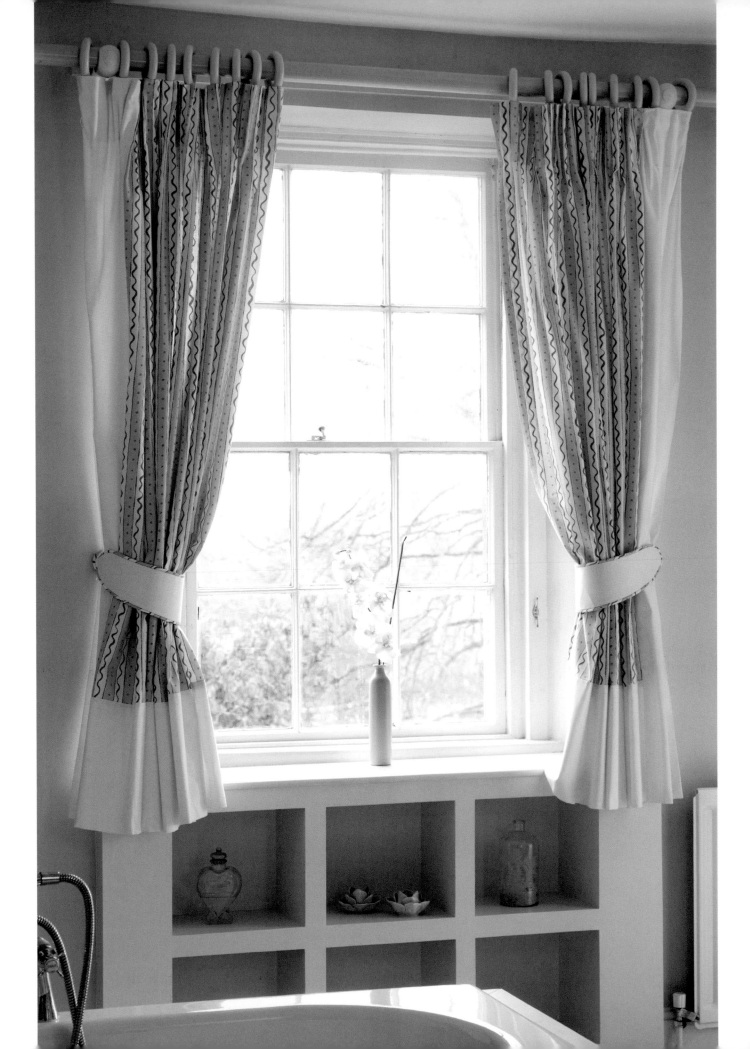

MAKING MATCHING TIEBACKS

1 Draw around the buckram tieback shape on the main fabric and add a ⅝in (1.5cm) seam allowance. Cut out four of these pieces from the main fabric and two from the fusible interfacing.

3 Make and attach a length of piping to the interfaced piece of each tieback, following steps 1–4 on pp. 54–55. Make sure you pin and stitch close to the edge of the buckram shape. Join the piping cord and fabric along the bottom edge of the tieback, as shown on p. 55.

FIGURE 7 ADD A SEAM ALLOWANCE TO THE TIEBACK SHAPE.

2 Centre one buckram tieback shape on the wrong side of one piece of fabric. Cover both with the interfacing and fuse together. Repeat for the other tieback.

FIGURE 8 FUSE THE INTERFACING TO THE FABRIC, TRAPPING THE BUCKRAM SHAPE.

FIGURE 9 PIN THE PIPING IN PLACE ON THE INTERFACED SIDE AND AROUND THE EDGE OF THE BUCKRAM SHAPE.

4 Snip into the seam allowances of the piping fabric to allow it to fit smoothly around the tieback shape. Press the raw edges over to the wrong side.

EXPERT TIP

WHEN FUSING THE BUCKRAM SHAPE BETWEEN THE FABRIC AND INTERFACING, USE A PRESSING CLOTH. THIS WILL ALLOW YOU TO USE A VERY HOT IRON ON ANY TYPE OF FABRIC.

FIGURE 10 PRESS THE EDGES TO THE WRONG SIDE.

5 Turn in the seam allowance all around the edges of the lining pieces, snipping into the curves to allow the fabric to lie flat. Press. Place a lining over the wrong side of one tieback. Pin around the edges and slip stitch the lining in place. Repeat to the other tieback. Sew two curtain rings to each tieback (see step 4 on p. 53).

USING THE BAGGING TECHNIQUE

THE TERM 'BAGGING' MEANS TO MACHINE STITCH CURTAIN FABRIC TO A LINING AROUND THE SIDE AND TOP EDGES. THIS 'BAG' IS THEN TURNED THROUGH. IT'S A QUICK AND EASY METHOD OF MAKING LINED CURTAINS.

THERE ARE TWO VARIATIONS ON THE METHOD — THE SEAMS JOINING THE TWO DIFFERENT FABRICS CAN EITHER LIE ALONG THE SIDE EDGES OR ON THE REVERSE OF THE CURTAIN — AND BOTH ARE EXPLAINED IN THIS CHAPTER.

BAGGING CHOICES

- Use the bagging method for any curtain that needs to be made quickly and easily.
- Bagged curtains are particularly suitable for the less traditional headings, such as tab tops, eyelets or clips.
- Bagging is a good option for making double-sided curtains, which look good from both sides and can also be reversed to ring the changes. In order to reverse curtains, the curtain header needs to look smart from both sides so a gathered casing, tab tops or eyelets are ideal, as shown in the Dramatic Double Vision project (pp. 66–71).
- Combine a fun print with a waterproof backing to make a practical shower curtain.

EXPERT TIP
FOR BEGINNERS, BAGGING WITH THE SEAMS ON THE REVERSE OF THE CURTAIN (SEE P. 64) IS THE EASIEST METHOD BECAUSE IT REQUIRES LESS PRECISION.

TOOLS AND EQUIPMENT
✓ Basic sewing kit (see p. 8)

BAGGING WITH SEAMS ON THE SIDE EDGES

This is the best option for a reversible curtain with two very different characters as only one fabric is visible on each side.

1 Join the main fabric panels to make up the full width as required for the curtain. If you are working with two furnishing fabrics for the front and reverse of the curtain, use flat fell seams to join the panels and reduce bulk (see p. 37). Press the seams well from the front and back. Join the panels for the lining in the same way.

2 Turn a 4in (10cm) double hem (8in (20cm) in total) along the bottom edge of the main fabric panel and press. Either hand stitch or machine blind stitch the hem in place. Turn the lining hem up by an extra ½in (1.25cm) so that it will be slightly shorter than the main fabric.

3 Measure up from the hem on the main fabric panel to the top of the curtain. On the wrong side, mark the required length across the width of the curtain with chalk or pencil. Allow a further 1in (2.5cm) seam allowance and then trim any excess fabric from the top edge.

FIGURE 1 TRIM THE EXCESS FABRIC FROM THE TOP OF THE CURTAIN.

4 Lay the two panels, right sides together, on a flat surface and smooth out any folds or creases. Pin across the top edge and down the side edges, checking that the lining is ½in (1.25cm) shorter than the main fabric. Sew the two layers together at the side seams and across the top. Trim the seam allowances and across the top corners.

WS

½in (1.25cm)

FIGURE 2 TRIM THE TOP CORNERS TO REDUCE BULK.

5 Press the seams flat. Then press the seam allowances open from the wrong side. Turn the curtain right sides out. Press the curtain, making sure the seams sit precisely along the edges.

FIGURE 3 PRESS THE SEAMS SO THEY LIE ALONG THE EDGES.

SEWING SENSE

For really crisp corners, use a point turner to push out the corners fully.

6 Finish this type of curtain with a casing (see pp. 35–36), tab tops (see pp. 42–44) or eyelets, as described in the Dramatic Double Vision project on pp. 66–71.

BAGGING WITH SEAMS ON THE REVERSE

Using this method, the lining is cut narrower than the main fabric so that when the curtain is laid flat, the main fabric folds to give contrast side edges on the reverse.

1 Make up the panels and hems on the main fabric and lining, following steps 1–3 on p. 63.

2 Trim the width of the lining so that it measures 6in (15cm) less than the width of the main fabric.

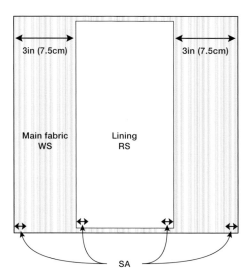

FIGURE 4 TAKE THE TURNINGS AND SEAM ALLOWANCES INTO ACCOUNT WHEN CUTTING THE PANELS.

3 Lay the main curtain flat, right side up. Place the lining centrally right side down over the curtain so that the lining hem is at least ½ in (1.25cm) above the bottom of the main curtain hem.

4 Pin and stitch one side edge of the main fabric and lining together, starting at the bottom. Repeat for the other side seam. As the lining is narrower, the main fabric will bag in the middle.

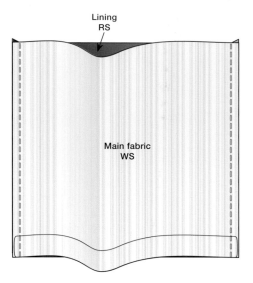

FIGURE 5 STITCH THE MAIN FABRIC AND LINING TOGETHER DOWN THE SIDE SEAMS.

5 Turn the curtain right sides out and press the side seams towards the lining. Smooth out the curtain so both borders are the same width. Pin and press the folded fabric.

FIGURE 6 MAKE SURE THE BORDERS ARE THE SAME WIDTH.

6 Finish the curtain header in the appropriate manner for the style of curtain.

AN EYELET HEADER TAPE GIVES A CONTEMPORARY LOOK TO
CURTAINS.

dramatic
DOUBLE-VISION CURTAINS

TWO TOTALLY DIFFERENT FABRICS
ENSURE THAT THESE CURTAINS USE THE
BAGGING TECHNIQUE VERY
EFFECTIVELY. THEY ARE FINISHED WITH
LARGE EYELETS, WHICH EASILY SLIDE
ALONG A CURTAIN POLE SO THE
CURTAINS CAN BE TURNED AROUND
QUICKLY TO GIVE A DRAMATICALLY
DIFFERENT LOOK.

THE EYELETS ARE CREATED WITH
SPECIAL RINGS ATTACHED THROUGH
HOLES MADE WITH THE HELP OF
EYELET HEADER TAPE. THE RINGS ARE
AVAILABLE IN VARIOUS COLOURS AND
METALLIC FINISHES.

FABRIC CALCULATION

1 Measure the curtain drop (see pp. 30–31) and then add:
- 8in (20cm for the hem
- 1in (2.5cm) for the header.

2 Measure the basic width across the window (see pp. 30–31) and then:
- multiply the measurement by 2¼ for fullness
- add an allowance for any seams and the side hems (see pp. 30–31).

3 Work out how many widths of fabric you need. Then multiply the total drop by the number of widths to give you the total length of fabric for one side of the curtain (see pp. 30–31).

YOU WILL NEED

✓ Two contrasting curtain fabrics (as calculated above)
✓ Basting tape or temporary adhesive (optional)
✓ 2–3 reels of matching thread
✓ Eyelet header tape (add 3in (7.5cm) to total width of each curtain)
✓ Large eyelet rings (9 rings for every 40in (1m) of tape)
✓ Basic sewing kit (see p. 8)
✓ Small scissors with very sharp points

TECHNICAL KNOW-HOW
Bagging curtains (see pp. 62–65)
Flat fell seaming (see p. 37)
Top stitching (see p. 19)

MATCHING STRIPES

If your fabric has distinctive vertical stripes, the curtain will look best if the stripes are matched carefully so that the overall pattern follows through across the panels. The following method ensures perfect matching of the pattern across the seams.

1 Fold the seam allowance under down one side edge and press. Apply basting tape (or temporary adhesive) along the folded seam allowance about ¼in (6mm) from the fold. Lap the folded seam allowance over the next panel, placing the fold against the seam line and ensuring that the pattern is matched perfectly.

Basting tape — — Seam line

FIGURE 1 USE BASTING TAPE TO HELP MATCH THE PATTERN.

2 Turn the panels so the wrong side is uppermost. Stitch the seam and then remove the basting tape.

EXPERT TIP
MAKE SURE THAT THE UPPER, CUT EDGE OF FABRIC IS LEVEL AND THE CUT CORNERS ARE EXACT RIGHT ANGLES USING A SET SQUARE. TRIM ANY EXCESS OFF BEFORE CUTTING THE PANELS AND MATCHING THE STRIPES.

PREPARING THE FABRIC

1 Cut the first panel of fabric, including the hem and header allowances. Cut the other panels to match. Cut the same number of panels of the second fabric to the same length.

2 Pin the curtain panels together to make the total width for each curtain. Repeat with the second fabric. Stitch all the seams using flat fell seams (see p. 37). Press.

SEWING SENSE
Trim the selvages or snip into them at regular intervals to ensure the seams hang straight.

3 Fold up a double hem of a total of 7½in (19cm) on the main fabric panels. Hand stitch or machine top stitch or blind hem in place. Repeat, making a double hem of 8in (20cm) on the second fabric panels. Set aside the second set of panels.

SEWING SENSE
If the fabric is thick, neaten the raw bottom edges with zigzag stitch. Then fold up a single hem of 4in (10cm) to reduce bulk.

4 Lay the main fabric panel flat, with the wrong side uppermost, and check the measurement from the finished hem to the top raw edge equals the drop required plus 1in (2.5cm). Mark the top edge of the curtain across the width with chalk or pins.

ATTACHING EYELET TAPE

1 Cut the eyelet tape to the required width of the curtain, making sure that there are an even number of holes and that the end holes are an equal distance from the ends of the tape.

2 With the wrong side of the main fabric panel uppermost, lap the lower edge of the eyelet tape over the top edge of the fabric so that the tape edge is along the marked chalk line. Stitch the tape to the fabric.

WS   RS

FIGURE 2 POSITION THE EYELET TAPE EDGE ALONG THE CHALK LINE BEFORE STITCHING THE TAPE TO THE FABRIC.

3 Fold the eyelet tape down to the wrong side of the curtain so that the fabric edge is folded over the top of the tape. Pin the tape in place.

EXPERT TIP
WHEN ATTACHING HEADER TAPE, USE A WALKING FOOT ON THE SEWING MACHINE TO PREVENT THE FABRIC FROM CREEPING UNDER THE TAPE.

4 Stitch the lower edge of the tape to the fabric, following the printed line on the tape.

5 Trim the ends of the tape so they sit just short of the seam lines on the fabric. Baste around all the holes in the header tape. Using small sharp scissors, carefully snip away the fabric inside each hole.

Basting

FIGURE 3 CUT AWAY THE FABRIC WITHIN EACH EYELET.

ATTACHING THE SECOND FABRIC

1 Lay the main curtain on a large surface with the right side uppermost. Smooth out the fabric, removing all folds and creases. Place the second curtain over it, right sides together and aligning the side seams. Make sure the hem on the second panel is ½in (1.25cm) higher than the hem on the main panel. Smooth out the second curtain.

2 Pin the two layers together along the side seams. Sew the side seams and press the seams flat. Then press the seam allowances open from the wrong side. Turn the curtain through and press it again so that the seams are down the side edges.

3 Lay the curtain flat and smooth. Pin the hems together. Fold the raw upper edge to the inside and level with the main fabric.

4 Pin or baste across the top edge of the curtain and then top stitch through all the layers.

EXPERT TIP
WHEN JOINING TWO CONTRASTING FABRICS TOGETHER, USE THREAD IN A COLOUR TO MATCH THE LOWER FABRIC IN THE BOBBIN AND THREAD TO MATCH THE TOP FABRIC IN THE NEEDLE.

FINISHING THE EYELETS

1 Baste the second fabric around the eyelets. With small, sharp scissors, cut away the excess fabric inside the eyelet holes on the second fabric.

EXPERT TIP
ALTERNATIVELY, WORK FROM THE RIGHT SIDE OF THE MAIN FABRIC AND TRIM THE SECOND FABRIC THROUGH THE EXISTING EYELET HOLES.

FIGURE 4 ATTACH THE METAL EYELETS TO FINISH THE CURTAIN.

2 Fix the eyelet rings through the holes, following the manufacturer's instructions and concealing the raw edges.

DRESSING UNUSUAL WINDOW SHAPES

WINDOWS WITH IRREGULAR SHAPES NEED VERY UNIQUE WINDOW DRESSINGS, WHICH WILL ADD A DISTINCT DESIGNER STYLE TO ANY ROOM. THE CURTAINS REQUIRE ACCURATE MEASUREMENTS AND SHAPING, ALL ACHIEVED BY MAKING CAREFULLY PREPARED TEMPLATES.

SHAPED WINDOWS CAN BE CIRCULAR OR TRIANGULAR, OR FEATURE AN ARCH OR APEX. WHATEVER THE SHAPE, WINDOW TREATMENTS CAN BE HUNG FROM A SPECIALLY SHAPED BATTEN USING ADHESIVE GRIP TAPE, AS WITH THE SHAPELY ARCHED WINDOW DRESSING (PP. 76–79).

TOOLS AND EQUIPMENT

✓ Curtain fabric
✓ Large sheets of paper, pencil and adhesive tape
✓ ¼in (6mm) plywood (width x depth of shaped part of window frame, plus 4in (10cm) all around)
✓ 2in (5cm) adhesive grip tape (to go around finished batten)
✓ Dual-purpose header tape (to go around shaped curtain edge)

SHAPELY CHOICES

- Add interest to small, plain windows by creating a shaped window dressing.
- Dress awkwardly shaped windows with sheers so that they don't need to be drawn back.
- Use tiebacks or Italian stringing on curtains that do need to be drawn back.

EXPERT TIP

IF THE SHAPED WINDOW HAS STRAIGHT SIDES, RODS CAN BE USED TO SUSPEND THE CURTAIN.

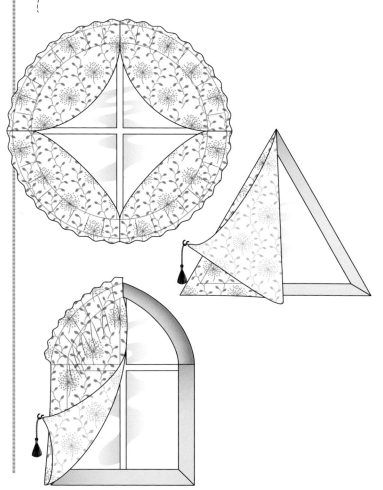

DRESSING APEX WINDOWS WITH SHEERS

If dressing an apex window with translucent sheers that remain closed, the simplest method is to hang the sheers from two rods fixed around the shaped section.

1 Make the sheers with casings, at least twice the width of window for fullness and with a drop from the top of the apex to the required length (see pp. 35–36 for making casings).

2 Feed the sheers onto the rods and let them hang for a few days. The sheers will hang to just longer than the correct length in the centre but much longer at the side edges. Carefully trim away the excess fabric from the bottom edge, leaving at least 4in (10cm) for hemming.

FIGURE 1 TRIM THE BOTTOM EDGE, LEAVING AN ALLOWANCE FOR THE HEM.

3 Take the sheers down. Turn the hem and hand stitch in place.

MAKING BATTENS AND PATTERNS FOR OTHER SHAPED WINDOWS

In order to maintain the unusual shape of a window, curtains for round, triangular or arched windows need to be fixed to a shaped batten or frame. Once the batten is in place, the measurements can be taken to create the curtain. These can be straight fabric panels, have simple pencil pleats or boxed pleats, although for small, shaped windows simple is best.

SPECIALIST TAPE

A specialist adhesive grip tape makes it much easier to dress a shaped window. The tape is available in various widths and has an adhesive backing, so it can be fixed to a batten, and a hook surface. The hooks attach themselves securely to dual-purpose header tape, which has a looped surface as well as the usual drawcords to pull it into shape. Therefore no curtain hooks, rings or tracks are required to hang the curtains. Different header styles are available, including classic pencil pleats, mini-pleats and net pleats.

EXPERT TIP

EVEN THOUGH THE GRIP TAPE HAS AN ADHESIVE BACKING, IT IS ADVISABLE TO STAPLE IT TO THE BATTEN IF USING A MEDIUM TO HEAVYWEIGHT FABRIC.

MAKING A BATTEN

1 Tape a large sheet of paper over the shaped area of the window. Draw around the shape of the window frame. Mark where the window frame starts to straighten out.

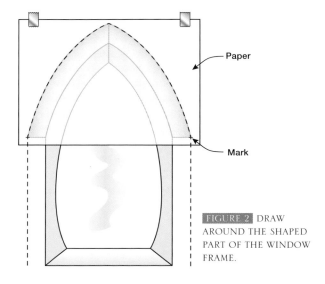

Paper

Mark

FIGURE 2 DRAW AROUND THE SHAPED PART OF THE WINDOW FRAME.

2 On the paper template, draw a parallel line 2in (5cm) outside
the first line. Square off the bottom edges of the shape. Use
the template to have the shape cut from plywood. Keep the
template for making a paper pattern for the curtains later. Fix the
plywood batten around the outside edge of the window frame.

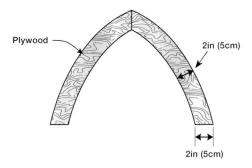

FIGURE 3 CUT THE SHAPE FROM PLYWOOD TO MAKE A BATTEN
FOR THE CURTAINS.

3 Peel the backing off the grip tape and stick it centrally along
the batten, notching it as necessary to follow the shape. If you
have a staple gun, also staple the tape in place.

4 Fix a cup hook to each side of the window frame about
halfway up and in line with the outer edges of the batten.

FIGURE 4 ATTACH THE GRIP TAPE AND FIX TWO CUP HOOKS.

CALCULATING THE FABRIC REQUIREMENTS

Having attached the batten from which the curtains will be
draped, you can take measurements to calculate the amount of
fabric needed.

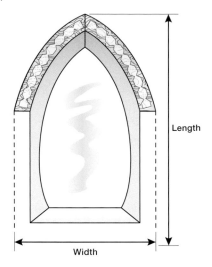

FIGURE 5 MEASURE THE DROP AND WIDTH FROM THE OUTSIDE
EDGES OF THE BATTEN.

1 For the total drop:
- measure from the highest point on the batten to the chosen
  hem length
- add a hem allowance
- add ¾in (2cm) for the header allowance
- add the pattern repeat (see p. 104) if applicable.

2 For the total width:
- measure from one outer edge of the batten to the other
- multiply that measurement by 2–2½ for fullness, depending
  on the header tape
- add allowances for side hems and seams.

3 Work out how may widths of fabric you need. Then multiply
the total drop by the number of widths to give you the total
length of fabric (see pp. 30–31).

MAKING A PATTERN FOR THE CURTAINS

Using the paper template made in steps 1 and 2 (see pp. 73–74) for making the batten, make a half pattern for each curtain, remembering to flip the pattern on the second curtain so that you get a left and a right-hand panel.

1 Lay the half-batten template on a larger sheet of paper and trace around the edges. Dispense with the template. Align a long ruler with the vertical edge at the highest point on the new pattern. Draw a line continuing that edge down the paper. Make another line, horizontally, continuing the bottom edge of the batten shape. The two new lines should cross.

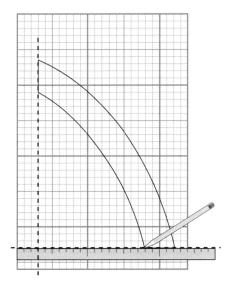

FIGURE 6 CONTINUE THE VERTICAL AND HORIZONTAL EDGES TO MAKE THE BASIC SHAPE FOR THE NEW PATTERN.

2 Divide the pattern into equal strips approximately 1¼in (3.25cm) wide and parallel to the vertical edge. Number the pieces in sequence from the longest to the shortest. Cut out the strips.

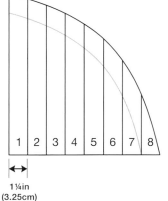

1 2 3 4 5 6 7 8

1¼in
(3.25cm)

FIGURE 7 NUMBER THE PAPER STRIPS IN SEQUENCE.

3 Use the paper pattern to cut out the fabric panels and make up the curtain as explained on p. 79.

IF DRESSING A SHAPED WINDOW, USE GRIP TAPE SO THAT YOU CAN FOLLOW THE SHAPE.

EXPERT TIP
FOR A ROUND WINDOW, CUT THE PATTERN STRIPS VERTICALLY FROM THE TOP TO THE BOTTOM OF THE CIRCULAR SHAPE.

shapely
ARCHED WINDOW DRESSING

THIS ARCHED WINDOW HAS BEEN
DRESSED WITH A FIXED CURTAIN,
ATTACHED WITH ADHESIVE GRIP TAPE
TO A SPECIALLY MADE BATTEN ON THE
WALL. THE METHOD FOR MAKING THE
BATTEN IS GIVEN ON PP. 73–74. WITH
ITS ATTRACTIVE LINING, THE CURTAIN
CAN THEN BE FLIPPED BACK TO LET IN
LIGHT. THIS TYPE OF DRESSING CAN
ALSO BE USED FOR TRIANGULAR OR
APEX-SHAPED WINDOWS.

FABRIC CALCULATION

1 Make a plywood batten as described on pp. 73–74. Fix it around the window frame. Apply adhesive grip tape as described on p. 74.

2 For the total drop:
- measure from the highest point on the batten to the chosen hem length
- add ¾in (2cm) for the hem allowance
- add ¾in (2cm) for the header allowance
- add the pattern repeat (see p. 104) if applicable.

3 For the total width:
- measure from one outer edge of the batten to the other
- multiply that measurement by 2–2½ for fullness, depending on the header tape
- add ¾in (2cm) for each side hem
- add allowances for any seams needed.

4 Work out how many widths of fabric you need. Then multiply the total drop by the number of widths to give you the total length of fabric (see pp. 30–31).

YOU WILL NEED
✓ Curtain fabric (as calculated above)
✓ Lining fabric (as curtain fabric)
✓ Batten (see pp. 73–74)
✓ 2in (5cm) adhesive grip tape (to go around shaped part of window)
✓ Paper pattern for top shaping (see p. 75)
✓ Dual-purpose header tape (to go around shaped edge of curtain)
✓ 2 x ½in (1.25cm) curtain rings
✓ 2 cup hooks

TECHNICAL KNOW-HOW
Dressing unusual shaped windows (see pp. 72–75)
Using adhesive grip tape (see p. 74)
Attaching header tape (see pp. 93–95)
Bagging (see pp. 62–65)

PIECING TOGETHER THE PANELS

1 With the right side uppermost, cut the first length of curtain fabric as a straight rectangle, including the hem and header allowances. Cut the rest of the panels, matching any pattern as necessary (see p. 105).

2 Piece together the fabric, using regular straight seams, to make the total width for both curtains, as yet without any shaping for the arch.

3 Repeat steps 1 and 2 to piece together the lining. Set the lining aside for the moment.

SHAPING THE TOP EDGE

1 Lay out one curtain, right side down, on a flat surface. Cut the paper pattern into strips (see p. 75 on making the basic pattern). Pin the first strip on the fabric so that the longest edge lies along the leading edge of the curtain and the top point sits where the top edge of the curtain will be (i.e. ¾in (2cm) from each raw edge). Using a long ruler, lightly mark a horizontal line across the fabric, continuing the bottom edge of the first pattern strip.

2 Pin the last pattern strip on the fabric so that its bottom edge sits on the marked line and its outer edge touches the outer edge of the curtain (i.e. ¾in (2cm) from the raw edge). Pin the rest of the strips in sequence along the marked line, leaving equal gaps between them.

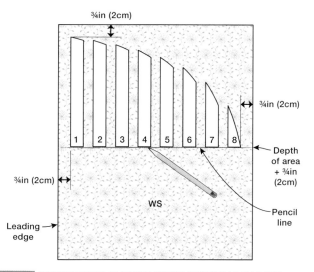

FIGURE 1 POSITION THE PATTERN STRIPS EVENLY ALONG THE BASE LINE.

3 Draw a smooth line joining the outer ends of the pattern. This will be the seam line. Then draw another line ¾in (2cm) outside the first. Dispense with the pattern pieces and cut along the second line.

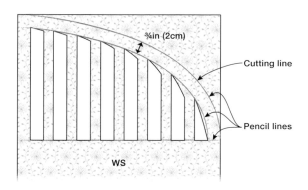

FIGURE 2 USE THE PATTERN PIECES AS A GUIDE TO CREATE THE SEAM AND CUTTING LINES.

4 Lay the cut curtain panel, right sides together, over the second panel. Smooth them out. Cut the second panel to match the first. Then shape the top of the two lining panels, making sure you cut a left and a right-hand panel.

5 With right sides together, stitch one panel of main fabric to the matching lining. Adapt the bagging technique on p. 63, by stitching around the side and bottom edges, leaving the top curved edge open. Trim the seams and corners. Turn the curtain right sides out and press. Repeat on the other curtain.

6 Press under ¾in (2cm) along all the curved edges. Pin or baste the curtain fabric and lining together along each curved edge.

7 Pin and stitch the top edge and ends of dual-purpose header tape along the top edge of each curtain. Pin and stitch the bottom edge of the tape in place, easing it as necessary.

FIGURE 3 EASE THE HEADER TAPE AROUND THE SHAPED TOP EDGE.

8 Stitch a curtain ring to the leading edge of each curtain anywhere from the centre to the bottom corner, depending on how you want the curtains to hang and how much light you want to allow in. Fix two cup hooks to the wall in line with the outside edge of the curtain.

9 Pull up the cords in the heading tape to fit the arch and attach the curtains to the batten. Hook the rings over the cup hooks to hold the curtains open.

SEWING WITH SHEERS

SHEERS ARE LIGHTWEIGHT, SEMI-TRANSPARENT FABRICS THAT LET THROUGH FILTERED LIGHT. THEY CAN BE USED INSTEAD OF CURTAINS ON WINDOWS THAT AREN'T OVERLOOKED OR AS AN ADDITIONAL LAYER OF WINDOW DRESSING. THE POPULAR CHOICE FOR SHEERS IS OFTEN VOILE.

SEWING WITH SHEERS CAN BE TRICKY BECAUSE THEY ARE SO LIGHTWEIGHT AND SLIPPERY. THEY ARE ALSO VISIBLE FROM BOTH SIDES SO SEAMS NEED TO BE ESPECIALLY NEAT. THIS CHAPTER SHOWS YOU HOW TO OVERCOME THESE POTENTIAL PROBLEMS AND THE VOLUPTUOUS VOILE CURTAINS (PP. 82–85) FEATURE A TAB TOP HEADING.

TOOLS AND EQUIPMENT

✓ Old sheet
✓ Basic sewing kit (see p. 8)

SHEER CHOICES

- Voile, a popular choice when sewing with sheers, looks like cotton lawn or organdie. It is usually made from cotton or synthetic fibres and is soft to handle. Traditionally white or cream, lots of different colours are now available, some with woven patterns or embroidered detail.
- Voiles work well gathered onto a pole. Transparent header tapes are available and are attached to the wrong side of curtain in the usual manner (see Using header tapes, pp. 92–97).
- Tab tops can be made of the same or contrasting fabric and finished with lightweight buttons or beading.
- Casings with ruffles of 1–2in (2.5–5cm) above the casing look attractive (see Making casings, pp. 35–36).
- Add a beaded trim to the leading edge, stitching it to the right side if the trim is on a decorative tape or to the reverse if it's on a plain tape.
- Attach sheers to the curtain pole with large rings or curtain clips.

CUTTING SHEERS

It is a good idea to take extra care when cutting sheers as the fabric has a tendency to slip away as you cut, especially if you have more than one layer. Avoid this by laying the fabric on an old sheet or other non-slip surface before cutting it. Preferably cut sheers as a single layer, but if you are cutting two layers, pin them together at very regular intervals just inside the cutting line. Also make sure your dressmaking shears are very sharp, which will stop the fabric catching on the blades.

EXPERT TIP

WHEN STRAIGHT STITCHING, PREVENT FINE FABRIC BEING PULLED DOWN INTO THE FEED DOGS BY REPLACING THE THROAT PLATE WITH A STRAIGHT STITCH PLATE, WHICH ONLY HAS A SMALL HOLE FOR THE NEEDLE AND IS SUPPLIED WITH MOST MODERN MACHINES.

SEWING SEAMS FOR SHEERS

Because sheers are translucent, any seams will show on both sides. One solution is to leave the selvages on the fabric and hang the fabric in loose floaty panels. Another solution is to use seams that are particularly suited to this type of fabric. French seams (see p. 36) conceal raw edges or the two seams described here are also ideal.

EXPERT TIP

WHEN SEWING SHEER FABRIC, USE A FINE NEEDLE (SIZE 9 (70)) AND A SMALL STITCH LENGTH, SUCH AS 2–2.2 (12–15 STITCHES PER INCH (2.5CM)).

HAIRLINE SEAM

This seam also conceals the raw edges. Unlike a French seam, it is suitable for curved edges as well as straight ones. However, it isn't a strong seam so is best avoided for seams that will come under stress.

1 With the wrong sides of the fabric together, sew a plain straight seam ½in (1.25cm) from the edge. Stitch again very close to the first stitches. Press. Trim the seam allowance very close to the stitching.

FIGURE 1 STITCH THE SECOND ROW OF STITCHES VERY CLOSE TO THE FIRST.

2 Turn, so the right sides are together and the seam is on the fold. Press. Using a narrow zigzag stitch approximately ⅛in (3mm) wide, stitch close to the edge, encasing the raw edges.

FIGURE 2 ENCASE THE RAW EDGES WITH ZIGZAG STITCH.

NARROW OVERCAST SEAM

This is also a very narrow seam that is better used on areas that do not come under stress.

1 With the right sides of the fabric together, sew a plain straight ⅝in (1.5cm) seam. Stitch again very close to the first stitches, and press.

2 Using a narrow zigzag stitch, stitch again close to the seam line. Trim the seam allowance very close to the zigzag stitch, and press.

FIGURE 3 TRIM THE SEAM ALLOWANCE VERY CLOSE TO THE STITCHING.

FABRIC CALCULATION

Because voiles are so lightweight, sheer curtains often have up to three times the fullness in the width. They are also sometimes left to puddle on the floor, for which an extra 16in (40.5cm) needs to be added to the length.

voluptuous VOILE CURTAINS

THESE DELICATE SHEERS FEATURE AN
OCCASIONAL EMBROIDERED STAR.
THEY USE SEAMS THAT ARE
PARTICULARLY SUITED TO
TRANSLUCENT FABRIC AND ARE HUNG
FROM FABRIC TABS, BUT ARE EASY TO
MAKE. THIS STYLE LOOKS WONDERFUL
AS FULL-LENGTH CURTAINS ALLOWED
TO PUDDLE ON THE FLOOR.

YOU WILL NEED

✓ Voile fabric (as calculated above)
✓ 2 reels of general-purpose
sewing thread
✓ Basic sewing kit (see p. 8)

TECHNICAL KNOW-HOW

Sewing seams for sheers (see p. 81)
Calculating fabric for curtains (see pp. 30–31)
Calculating fabric for tabs (see pp. 42–43)
Working with patterned fabric (see pp. 102–105)

FABRIC CALCULATION

1 Measure the curtain drop (see p. 30) and then add:
- 4in (10cm) for the top turning
- 4in (10cm) for the hem
- 16in (40.5cm) for the puddle look
- any pattern repeat (see p. 104).

2 Measure the basic width across the window (see p. 30) and then:
- triple the measurement for fullness
- add an allowance for seams (see p. 30)
- add ¾in (2cm) for each side hem (see p. 30).

3 Work out how many widths of fabric you need. Then multiply the total drop by the number of widths to give you the total length of fabric for the basic curtains (see p. 31).

4 Add on the amount of fabric needed for the tabs (although you may be able to cut these from off-cuts of the main curtain fabric). The finished tabs on the curtains shown here are 2in (5cm) wide and 8in (20cm) long, with approximately 8in (20cm) between each tab. Follow the calculations for tabs on pp. 42–43, but allow for the fabric being folded lengthwise to make each tab and for only ½in (1.25cm) for each seam.

FIGURE 1 MULTIPLY THE AMOUNT OF FABRIC REQUIRED FOR EACH TAB BY THE NUMBER OF TABS YOU NEED.

5in (12.5cm)

½in (1.25cm)

9in (23cm)

Fold

½in
(1.25cm)

PREPARING SHEERS FOR TAB TOPS

1 With the right side uppermost, cut the first panel of fabric, including the allowances. (See p. 81 for advice on cutting sheer fabric.) Cut the remaining panels, matching any pattern repeat as necessary (see p. 105).

2 Pin the panels together, matching the pattern, to make the total width for each curtain. Sew any seams, using French Seams (see p. 36) or narrow overcast seams (see p. 81).

3 Turn under the raw edges by ³⁄₈in (1cm) once, and then again to make a double hem down each side edge. Machine stitch in place and press.

EXPERT TIP

If selvages are neat and don't distort the fabric, leave them as the side edges.

4 Turn up the bottom edge by 2in (5cm) once, and then again to make a double hem. Top stitch the hem in place close to the top fold. Press.

MAKING AND ATTACHING THE TABS

1 Cut the fabric for the required number of tabs. Fold each piece in half lengthways, right sides together, and stitch a ¹⁄₂in (1.25cm) straight seam down the long side. Turn the tabs right sides out and press with the seam in the centre or down one edge.

SEWING SENSE

Make up several tabs so that you can work out exactly how many are required.

2 Fold each tab in half with the raw short edges together. Pin ¹⁄₂in (1.25cm) from the raw edges.

3 With the right side uppermost, place a row of pins across the top of the curtain 4in (10cm) from the raw edge. Position a tab at each side edge of the curtain, letting the loop hang down and lining up the pins on the tabs with the pins on the curtains. Pin the remaining tabs evenly along the pinned line.

FIGURE 2 USE TWO PINS TO SECURE EACH TAB SO THE FABRIC DOESN'T SLIP.

EXPERT TIP

USE THE SPAN OF YOUR HAND TO MEASURE THE SPACES AND POSITION THE TABS QUICKLY. THEN ADJUST AS NECESSARY.

4 Check the entire length of the curtain, including the tabs, and adjust the level of the pins on the curtain if necessary.

EXPERT TIP

IF YOU HAVE TO SHORTEN THE CURTAIN, CUT THE EXCESS OFF THE MAIN CURTAIN, NOT OFF THE TABS.

5 Turn up the tabs, folding the top turning on the main curtain to the wrong side. Fold the turning over twice, enclosing all the raw edges. Pin, then top stitch the top and bottom edges of the turning in place through all the layers.

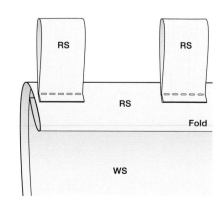

FIGURE 3 FOLD THE TURNING OVER TO ENCLOSE THE RAW EDGES.

6 Slot the pole through the tabs, adjust the gathers and hang the curtains in place.

MAKING PERFECT POCKETS

POCKETS CAN BE ADDED TO SOFT FURNISHINGS AS WELL AS TO CLOTHING. FOR FURNISHINGS, THE MOST COMMONLY USED IS A PATCH POCKET — ONE THAT IS SEWN ON TOP OF THE FABRIC AS A PATCH.

POCKETS CAN BE PURELY PRACTICAL OR THEY CAN BE VERY DECORATIVE, DEPENDING ON THE FABRICS AND TECHNIQUES USED. HERE WE GIVE INSTRUCTIONS FOR MAKING RECTANGULAR POCKETS, BUT ONCE YOU KNOW THE BASICS, WHY NOT EXPLORE DIFFERENT SHAPED POCKETS WITH GATHERS OR PLEATS? HAVE FUN MAKING ALL KINDS OF POCKETS FOR CURTAINS, INCLUDING THE DELICATE VOILES ON PP. 88—91.

TOOLS AND EQUIPMENT
✓ Paper and pencil
✓ Basic sewing kit (see p. 8)

POCKET CHOICES
- Make pockets from the main curtain or contrasting fabric. Try sheers and solid blocks of colour in any combination.
- Try different shapes of pocket – circles and triangles work well.
- Incorporate gathers or pleats into the top and/or bottom edges of the pockets.
- Close them with hook and loop tape, buttons or toggles.

MAKING A BASIC POCKET
The most basic pocket is a rectangular patch sewn onto the front of background fabric. They are easy to make and attach to curtains and other soft furnishings.

1 First make a paper pattern. Using pen and paper, draw the outline for the size and shape of pocket you want. Add turning allowances of ⅝in (1.5cm) on the side and bottom edges. Add a deep heading allowance of 1¼–3in (3.25–7.5cm) on the top edge. Cut out around the outer edges of the pattern.

2 Pin the pattern to the fabric, making sure it lies on the straight grain, so the finished pocket will not stretch out of shape. Cut out the pocket.

EXPERT TIP
IF USING A LIGHTWEIGHT (BUT NOT TRANSPARENT) FABRIC, INTERFACE THE WRONG SIDE OF THE POCKET WITH A FUSIBLE INTERFACING CUT TO THE FINISHED SIZE.

3 Turn under the side and bottom edges by ⅝in (1.5cm) and press them in place. Lightweight fabric will turn under neatly. However, if using medium- or heavyweight fabric, mitre the corners (see pp. 20–21).

EXPERT TIP
CUT A CARD TEMPLATE THE SIZE OF THE FINISHED POCKET. YOU CAN USE IT TO CUT LOTS OF POCKET PIECES AND AS A GUIDE TO TURN UNDER THE SEAM ALLOWANCES.

4 Turn under the allowance for the top edge and then tuck the raw edge under again by ⅜in (1cm). Top stitch the allowance in place close to the bottom fold.

5 Pin the pocket to the main fabric. Edge stitch it in place ⅛in (3mm) from the side and bottom edges. Reinforce the pocket by stitching around the top corners in a triangle. Press.

FIGURE 1 REINFORCE THE POCKET AT THE TOP CORNERS TO PREVENT IT BEING PULLED AWAY FROM THE MAIN FABRIC.

LINING POCKETS

Λ lining adds weight and stability to a pocket and provides a neat finish on the inside.

1 Cut the lining the same size as the pocket with seam allowances. Mark the foldline for the top turning. With right sides together, stitch the lining to the main fabric along the top edge, leaving an opening for turning. Press the seam allowance open.

FIGURE 2 STITCH AROUND THE EDGES, SECURING THE TOP TURNING IN THE SIDE SEAMS.

2 Turn the top allowance down to the lining side. Aligning the raw edges, stitch the side and bottom edges of the lining and main fabric together. Trim across the corners.

3 Turn the pocket right sides out. Slip stitch the opening closed. Press, and top stitch across the top of the pocket if desired. Attach the pocket to the main fabric as in step 5 above.

SHAPING CURVED POCKETS

A common variation for the rectangular patch pocket is to have curved bottom corners.

1 Cut out the pocket in the usual way. Using a small plate or saucer, draw a smooth curved line around one bottom corner, joining the side and bottom seams. Fold the fabric in half lengthwise and cut away the excess fabric on both corners. Mark the new seam line around the corners.

2 Stitch along the seam line, taking care to stay on the line around the curved corners. Notch across the seam allowance around the curves to reduce bulk and so the finished curves will be smooth and neat.

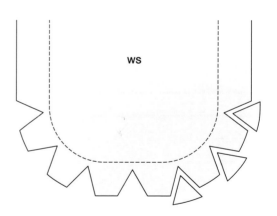

FIGURE 3 SNIP ACROSS THE SEAM ALLOWANCE AROUND THE CURVES.

SEWING SENSE
Outer curves are notched by cutting wedges out of the seam allowance. When turned through, the wedges close up without adding bulk in the seams.

3 Turn the seam allowance to the wrong side so stitched line is just turned under and press. Attach the pocket in the usual way.

surprise POCKET VOILES

THIS PAIR OF VOILES IS FULL OF
SURPRISES, BUT USES TECHNIQUES YOU
HAVE ALREADY COME ACROSS IN THIS
BOOK. THERE IS A CASING AT THE TOP
SO THE CURTAINS ARE EASY TO SLIP
ONTO A POLE. THE MAIN FEATURE ARE
SCATTERED POCKETS, WHICH CAN BE
FILLED WITH SWEET-SMELLING POT
POURRI, FAUX FLOWER HEADS OR ANY
OTHER FAVOURITE TRINKETS AND
TREATS. TO COMPLETE THE ROMANTIC
LOOK, THESE VOILES ARE EXTRA-LONG
SO THEY BILLOW IN THE BREEZE AND
PUDDLE ON THE FLOOR.

FABRIC CALCULATION

1 Measure the curtain drop (see p. 30). Then add:
- the pole circumference, plus 3in (7.5cm) for ease and turning the casing allowance
- 4in (10cm) for the hem
- 16in (40.5cm) for the puddle look.

2 Measure the basic width across the window (see p. 30). Then:
- triple the measurement for fullness
- add an allowance for seams
- add 1in (2.5cm) for each side hem.

3 Work out how many widths of fabric you need. Then multiply the total drop by the number of widths to give you the total length of fabric for the basic curtains (see pp. 30–31).

YOU WILL NEED

- ✓ Voile fabric (as calculated above)
- ✓ ¼yd (25cm) voile or contrast fabric for pockets, depending on size and number
- ✓ 2 reels of general-purpose sewing thread
- ✓ Basic sewing kit (see p. 8)

TECHNICAL KNOW-HOW

Calculating fabric requirements (see pp. 30–31)
Top stitching (see p. 19)
Making casings (see pp. 35–36)
Making pockets (see p. 87)

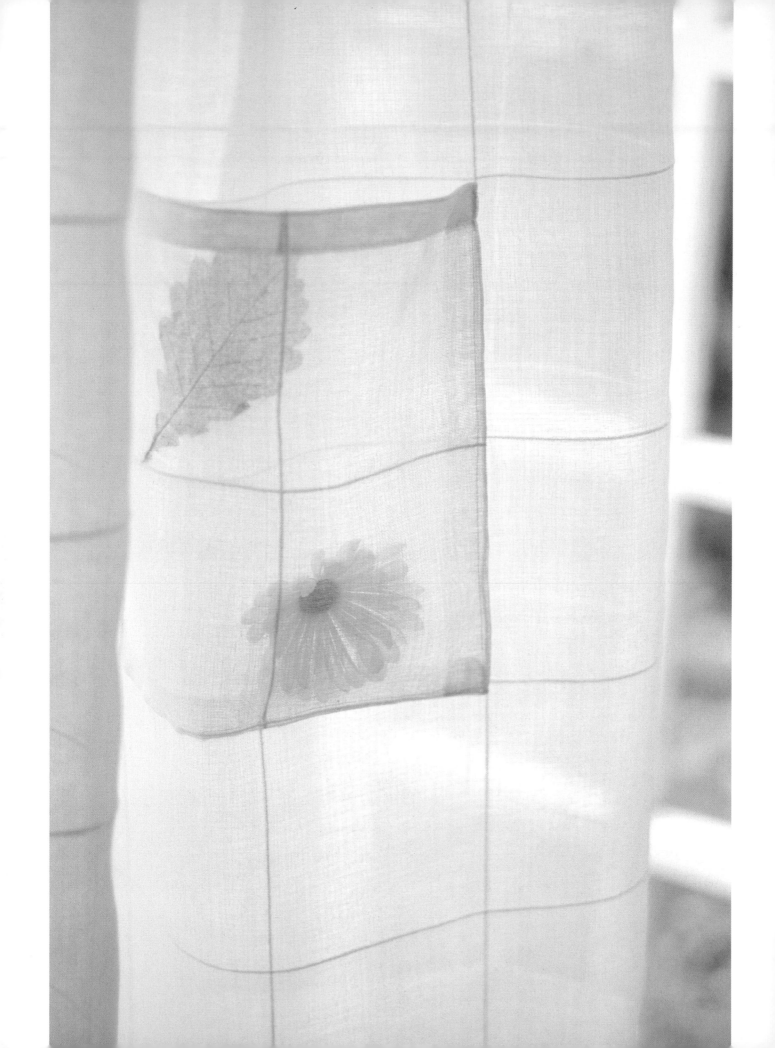

MAKING THE MAIN PANELS

1 Cut the panels. In the curtains shown below right, the panels have been left to hang independently by just hemming the sides with a double hem of ³⁄₈in twice. If preferred, you can join the panels with French seams, (see p. 36) and turn double hems down the side edges, machine stitching them in place. Press.

2 Turn under 2in (5cm) once, and then again to make a double hem along the bottom edge. Top stitch the hem in place close to the top fold. Press.

EXPERT TIP

USE A SIZE 9 (70) UNIVERSAL NEEDLE FOR SEWING VOILE.

3 Measure up from the hemmed bottom edge and mark along the desired finished top edge of the curtain on the wrong side of the fabric. Fold the top turning allowance to the wrong side and press the fold in place to crease.

MAKING THE CASING

1 Take half the circumference of the pole and add 1in (2.5cm) for ease. Use that measurement to mark another line parallel to the top turning and closer to the raw edge. Fold the raw edge under along the new line.

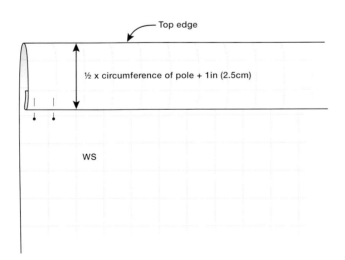

Top edge

½ x circumference of pole + 1in (2.5cm)

WS

FIGURE 1 FOLD THE CASING ALLOWANCE WITH ENOUGH FABRIC TO EASE OVER THE POLE.

2 Check the casing is wide enough for the pole and then machine stitch again close to the top, approximately ³⁄₈in (1cm) from the edge. Press. Finish it as explained on p. 35.

SEWING SENSE

Stitch the casing from the wrong side so that you can see clearly that the raw edge is secured by the stitching.

MAKING THE POCKETS

1 Make and attach the desired number of pockets as explained on pp. 86–87. Press the curtains.

2 Fill the pockets with petals, flower heads or pot pourri. Slot the pole into the casing, adjust the gathers and hang the voiles in place.

USING DIFFERENT CURTAIN HEADERS

CURTAINS CAN BE GATHERED AND PLEATED ALONG THE TOP EDGE IN A VARIETY OF DIFFERENT HEADER STYLES, WHICH MAKE THEM DRAPE IN BEAUTIFUL FOLDS. FROM THE INFORMALITY OF A SIMPLY GATHERED HEADER TO THE TRADITIONAL PENCIL, BOX OR GOBLET PLEATS, THERE'S A READY-MADE HEADER TAPE TO MAKE THE PROCESS EASY.

THIS CHAPTER EXPLAINS HOW TO USE THESE TAPES AND ALSO HOW TO MAKE PINCH PLEATS USING BUCKRAM RATHER THAN HEADER TAPE. THE PROJECT ON PP. 98—101 SHOWS HOW TO COMBINE PINCH PLEATS WITH A LINED CURTAIN TO GIVE A VERY PROFESSIONAL FINISH.

TOOLS AND EQUIPMENT

✓ Basic sewing kit (see p. 8)
✓ Header tape of your choice or buckram

HEADER CHOICES

- Deep pencil pleats are suitable for most types of fabric, except nets and very lightweight voiles. They produce a luxurious effect and look well on full, floor-length curtains. Header tapes are also available to make standard pencil pleats, pinch pleats and mini-pleats on shorter curtains and short pencil pleats on voiles and nets.
- Pinch pleats are arranged in evenly spaced groups of three pleats across the curtain top, with flat areas of fabric between each group. They are also suitable for all fabric types except very lightweight ones.
- Box pleats give a very crisp, tailored look and are particularly useful for shorter fixed curtains, valances or unusually shaped windows. They look best with medium to lightweight fabric.
- Goblet pleats are a variation of pinch pleats (and there are various others). The pleats are held in place at the bottom of the header, but above them the fabric opens out to form a goblet shape.

EXPERT TIP

VISIT A SOFT FURNISHINGS STORE OR DEPARTMENT TO LOOK AT DIFFERENT HEADERS ON SAMPLE CURTAINS. THIS WILL HELP YOU TO DECIDE WHICH TYPE YOU PREFER.

IDENTIFYING PARTS OF HEADER TAPE

Header tape produces a stiff, robust set of gathers or pleats along the top edge of curtain fabric. The effect is achieved when the tape is gathered up along the cords in the tape and the curtains are then hung up from hooks attached to the tape.

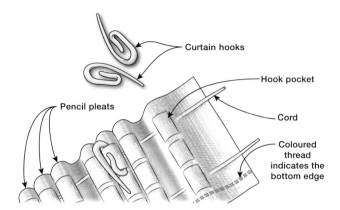

FIGURE 1 USE HEADER TAPE FOR PENCIL PLEATS FOR MANY DIFFERENT TYPES OF FABRIC AND CURTAIN.

CALCULATING FABRIC REQUIREMENTS

To achieve a pleated effect, you need 2–3½ times the window width for fullness. The precise amount of fullness depends on the type of header tape, and advice will usually be marked on the tape. Tight pencil pleats usually require 3–3½ times the window width – more fullness than other styles. Pinch and goblet pleats usually require 2–2½ times the window width, while box pleats need 3 times the amount.

When calculating the complete drop of the fabric for each curtain panel, add double the depth of the header tape, plus ¼in (6mm), for the header allowance.

See pp. 30–31 for more details on calculating fabric requirements. If you are using buckram instead of header tape, see the advice on pp. 96–97.

Your choice of header will also have an impact on the weight of the fabric you use. Heavyweight fabrics are better teamed with header tapes that require 2–2½ fullness, whereas medium and lightweight fabrics can be gathered up to 3½ times to give a full, rich look.

CALCULATING THE LENGTH OF HEADER TAPE

Add ½yd (50cm) to the total width of fabric for each curtain so that you have enough tape to position the pleats where you want to along the top of the curtain.

PREPARING THE CURTAINS AND HEADER TAPE

Attaching the header tape is almost the last process in curtain making. First, sew together the fabric panels, hem the side edges, make and attach the linings and baste the bottom hems in place (pp. 129–130).

1 Check the measurements of the curtains from the hem to the top edge against the original requirements. Mark the top edge of the finished curtain, which should leave enough fabric for a turning of double the depth of the header tape, plus ¼in (6mm). Any other excess of fabric can be cut off. Fold a turning the depth of the tape plus ⅛in (3mm) once, and then again.

Depth of header tape + ⅛in (3mm)

RS

WS

FIGURE 2 FOLD A DOUBLE TURNING ALONG THE TOP EDGE OF THE CURTAIN.

2 Cut the tape to length for each curtain, allowing up to ½yd (50cm) more than the width of the full curtain, depending on the type of tape. Taking the end of the tape that will be on the leading edge of each curtain, pull 2in (5cm) of each cord free from the tape and knot each cord securely. Trim the excess tape to about 1in (2.5cm) and turn it under.

FIGURE 3 KNOT THE CORDS SECURELY.

SEWING SENSE
Remember that there are two leading edges on a pair of curtains – one on the right edge of the left-hand curtain, the other on the left edge of the right-hand curtain.

POSITIONING PENCIL PLEAT TAPE

1 Ensure the tape is the correct way up and the hook pockets are facing you. Starting at the leading edge, pin the header tape so that it starts with a row of hook pockets at the end and sits about 1/8in (3 mm) from the top edge of the curtain. Continue to pin the tape across the top edge.

2 At the other end of the tape, pull 2in (5cm) of each cord free from the tape beyond the edge of the curtain so that you can use them to pull up the pleats later. Trim the excess tape to about 1in (2.5cm) and tuck it under. Continue to pin the tape around the remaining edges.

FIGURE 4 PIN THE HEADER TAPE IN POSITION ABOUT 1/8IN (3MM) BELOW THE TOP EDGE OF THE CURTAIN.

POSITIONING PINCH, BOX AND GOBLET PLEAT TAPE

These types of pleats are interspersed with flat areas of fabric and the curtains hang best if there is a flat area of fabric at each end of the header.

1 Find the centre of the cut length of header tape. With the hook pockets uppermost, insert a pin through the centre of pleat section nearest the centre of the tape. Use another pin to mark the centre of the flat area between pleats nearest the centre of the tape. Finally mark the centre of the curtain panel along the top edge.

FIGURE 5 FIND THE CENTRE OF THE CENTRAL PLEAT AND FLAT SECTION OF THE TAPE.

2 Line up each of the pins on the tape with the one on the curtain to see which one leaves the most flat tape at the sides of the curtain. Choose the best match and pin the tape to the curtain as in steps 1–2, left.

FIGURE 6 MATCH THE PINS THAT ALLOW FOR A FLAT SECTION OF TAPE AT EACH SIDE OF THE CURTAIN.

SEWING SENSE

If you pull any cords out of the tape, use a fine crochet hook to pull them back through the tape.

ATTACHING HEADER TAPE

Using the machine, straight stitch the tape in place close to the edges. Start at the bottom left corner, continuing up the side, along the top edge and down the opposite side to the bottom right, pivoting at the corners and keeping the cords out of the way. Start stitching again to attach the bottom edge, but stitching from the left to the right, to prevent the header tape from twisting.

Lining WS

FIGURE 7 ATTACH THE TAPE ALONG THE SIDE AND TOP EDGES FIRST, BEFORE STITCHING ALONG THE BOTTOM EDGE IN THE SAME DIRECTION AS YOU STITCHED THE TOP.

FORMING PENCIL PLEATS

1 Securely hold onto the free ends of the cords with one hand. With the other hand, gently push the heading along the cords, away from the loose ends, so that the fabric is pleated to the maximum extent and the pleats are set.

FIGURE 8 HOLD THE CORDS AND PUSH THE HEADING AWAY TO FORM THE PLEATS.

2 Ease the heading out again until the curtain is the correct width. Tie a slip knot in the loose cords. Do not cut the cords because the heading will need to be pulled back out if the curtains need to be stored or cleaned.

EXPERT TIP
CURTAINS HANG BETTER IF YOU LEAVE A FLAT AREA ON EACH SIDE EDGE, RATHER THAN GATHERING THE FABRIC RIGHT TO THE EDGE.

EXPERT TIP
ADJUST THE PLEATS AS NECESSARY TO GIVE A UNIFORM APPEARANCE.

FORMING PINCH AND BOX PLEATS

Hold the cords as for pencil pleats. Push the first set of pleats into position. Then push the second set into position. Return to the first set, which will have come out, and reform those pleats. Repeat across the whole curtain. Secure the cords as explain in step 1 above.

FORMING GOBLET PLEATS

Hold the top cord and push the top part of the first goblet into position. Then pull the bottom cord so the first two pleats meet to form the stem below the goblet shape. Push the finished goblet along the heading and form the next one in the same way. Return to the first goblet again. Repeat, until the whole curtain is pleated with goblets. Secure the cords as before.

STITCHING PINCH AND GOBLET PLEATS

Secure the pleats on the front on the curtain, overstitching them together just below the tape. You could add buttons, braid or beads to hide the stitching and then add decorative detail.

FIGURE 9 OVERSTITCH THE PLEATS JUST BELOW THE TAPE.

HANGING THE CURTAINS

There are various styles of curtain hook, some of them for specific types of header tape. Attach them in the row of pockets that best suits the type of support you are using. For example, the middle or bottom row is usually best for a curtain pole so that the top of the curtain is close to the pole.

FIGURE 10 INSERT CURTAIN HOOKS CLOSE TOGETHER TO SUPPORT THE PLEATS.

USING BUCKRAM INSTEAD OF HEADER TAPE

Buckram is a stiffener that can be used to make curtain headings instead of using ready-made header tape. It is available in different widths to cater for pleats of varying depths. Choose wider buckram for long curtains with a deep pleated header or narrower buckram for shorter curtains. Buckram works well on lined curtains as it is hidden between the layers of fabric. You will need to cater for its use in your fabric calculations. Each pleat takes up 4¾in (12cm) of fabric; each flat area between the pleats takes the same amount, and you will need to allow for one more flat area than the number of pleats.

This method can be adapted to make any type of header you want. Steps 1–6 describe how to make goblet or pinch pleats using buckram, but first prepare the curtains and the linings, stitching the side hems and basting the bottom hems. Do not attach the lining yet.

1 Cut a length of buckram to match the width of the finished curtain. Check the measurements of the curtain from the hem to the top edge against the original requirements. Mark the top edge, which should leave enough fabric for a turning of the depth of the heading. Cut off any other excess of fabric.

2 Fold down the top turning so that the curtain is the correct length. Slip the buckram under the turning and pin it in place. Place the lining, wrong sides together, on top of the curtain, folding the top raw edge of the lining under so it sits just below the top of the main curtain. Hand stitch across the top, catching the lining to the curtain.

3 With the lining uppermost, mark C on the central point along the top edge of the curtain. Working from the centre, mark one point 2⅜in (6cm) on each side of centre. Then mark along the top edge at 4¾in (12cm) intervals to map out the positions of the pleats and flat areas between them. Make sure there is a flat area at each side edge of the curtain. Link the pleat markings so you do not confuse them with the flat areas.

FIGURE 11 CAREFULLY MARK OUT THE PLEATS AND FLAT AREAS.

4 Working from the back of the curtain, bring the first pleat markings together to form a tube on the right side of the curtain. Pin and stitch the tube in place through all the thicknesses from the top to the bottom of the buckram. Repeat for all the other pleats. If making goblet pleats, go to step 7 below.

FIGURE 12 SECURE THE FIRST FOLD WITH STITCHING.

5 For three pinch pleats, lay the curtain on a flat surface, right side up, so the tube shapes stand proud. Holding one tube in one hand, pinch the fabric halfway from the front fold to the seam and push in towards the seam so that three pleats are formed.

FIGURE 13 PUSH THE TUBE SHAPE TOWARDS THE SEAM TO FORM THREE PLEATS.

6 On the front of the curtain, overstitch the pleats together by hand just below the buckram, as shown on p. 96.

7 For goblet pleats, pinch and push in the tube to form small pleats at the bottom on the tube. Overstitch the pleats by hand to secure them just below the buckram.

HANGING THE CURTAINS

To attach the curtains to a pole, you will need to use pin hooks. Turn the curtain to the back and insert one pin hook, using the sharp, pointed end to pierce all the layers except the main curtain fabric slightly to the side of each pleat seam.

FIGURE 14 PUSH THE SHARP POINT OF THE PIN HOOK THROUGH THE LINING AND BUCKRAM.

A TRIPLE-PLEAT HEADER PROVIDES A CLASSIC, STYLISH FINISH TO A LONG CURTAIN.

perfect PINCH PLEAT CURTAINS

PINCH PLEATS, ALSO CALLED TRIPLE
PLEATS, GIVE A VERY PROFESSIONAL
FINISH TO THESE LINED CURTAINS,
WHICH CASCADE IN SOFT FOLDS AS
THEY FALL TO THE FLOOR. THIS STYLE
IS PARTICULARLY SUITED TO FULL-
LENGTH CURTAINS, BUT IS EASY TO
ACHIEVE. THE LINING IS ATTACHED
USING THE BAGGING METHOD, WHICH
CUTS DOWN ON THE AMOUNT OF
HAND STITCHING. YOU CAN TRIM THE
PLEATS WITH MATCHING OR
CONTRASTING FABRIC-COVERED
BUTTONS IF YOU WISH.

FABRIC CALCULATION

1 Measure the curtain drop (see p. 30) and then add:
- 8in (20cm) for the hem
- double the depth of the header tape, plus ¼in (6mm)
- the pattern repeat (see p. 104).

2 Measure the basic width across the window (see p. 30) and then:
- double the measurement for fullness
- add an allowance for seams (see p. 30)
- add 6in (15cm) per curtain for the side seams and facings.

EXPERT TIP

ADD 4¾IN (12CM) TO THE WIDTH IN EACH CURTAIN SO
THAT THEY OVERLAP WHEN CLOSED, AS THIS TYPE OF
HEADING HAS A TENDENCY TO SPRING BACK FROM THE
LEADING EDGE.

3 Work out how many widths of fabric you need. Then multiply the total drop by the number of widths to give you the total length of fabric (see pp. 30–31).

YOU WILL NEED

✓ Curtain fabric (as calculated above)
✓ Lining fabric (as curtain fabric, minus any pattern repeat allowance)
✓ Pinch pleat header tape (add ½yd (50cm) to total width of each curtain)
✓ 2–3 reels of general-purpose sewing thread
✓ Basic sewing kit (see p. 8)

TECHNICAL KNOW-HOW

Bagging with seams on the reverse (see p. 64)
Using header tapes (see pp. 92–97)
Making a lining (see pp. 129–131)

PREPARING THE CURTAINS

1 With the right side uppermost, cut the first length of curtain fabric, including the hem and header allowances but not the pattern repeat. Cut the remaining panels, matching the pattern as necessary (see p. 105).

2 Cut the panels of lining to the length of the first panel of curtain fabric (see pp. 129–131 on linings). Leave to one side.

3 Pin the curtain fabric panels together, matching the pattern repeat, to make the total width for each curtain. Sew any seams, using regular straight seams and machine sewing from hem to top. Neaten the seam allowances with overcast or zigzag stitch (see p. 18). Press the seams.

4 Turn up the bottom hem allowance by 4In (10cm) once, and then again to make a double hem. Do not stitch the hem, but press and pin it in place.

5 Fold over the raw edges by 3in (7.5cm) down each side of the curtain and press. Check and note the total width of the curtain.

PREPARING THE LINING

1 Piece the lining together in the same way as the main fabric. Turn up the bottom hem in the same way, but machine stitch it in place.

2 Measure and mark the lining panel 6in (15cm) less wide than the main fabric. Cut off the excess.

FIGURE 1 CUT THE LINING 6IN (15CM) LESS WIDE THAN THE MAIN FABRIC.

3 With the main fabric right side up, place the lining right side down on top. Position the bottom of the lining at least 2in (5cm) above the bottom edge of the main fabric. Pin and stitch the two side edges of main fabric and lining together, starting from the bottom hems. It will seem strange as the lining is narrower than the main fabric, but this is correct.

FIGURE 2 STITCH THE MAIN FABRIC AND LINING TOGETHER DOWN THE SIDE SEAMS.

4 Turn the curtain right sides out and press the side seams towards the lining. Smooth out the curtain so both borders are the same width. Pin and press the folds.

FIGURE 3 MAKE SURE THE BORDERS ARE THE SAME WIDTH.

ATTACHING HEADER TAPE

1 Check the measurements of the curtain from the hem to the top edge against the original requirements. Mark the top edge of the finished curtain, which should leave enough fabric for a turning of double the depth of the header tape, plus ¼in (6mm). Trim away any excess fabric. Fold a turning the depth of the tape plus ⅛in (3mm) once, and then again (see Fig. 2 on p. 93).

2 Continue attaching the header, following the instructions on pp. 93–96.

WORKING WITH PATTERNED FABRIC

ONE OF THE BEST THINGS ABOUT MAKING CURTAINS YOURSELF IS THAT YOU CAN REALLY TRANSFORM THE LOOK OF THE ROOM BY INTRODUCING A PATTERNED FABRIC THAT COORDINATES WITH YOUR DÉCOR. PAGES 106–111 SHOW YOU HOW TO MAKE STYLISH FLOOR-LENGTH PATTERNED CURTAINS FEATURING DECORATIVE GOBLET PLEATS. WORKING WITH A PATTERNED FABRIC PRESENTS SOME CHALLENGES, SO BEFORE YOU PICK A PRINT, HERE ARE A FEW USEFUL TIPS AND TECHNIQUES.

FABRIC CHOICES

· The trick to making a patterned fabric look fresh and modern is to use it sparingly and team it with simple accessories. For instance, keep the walls plain and you can have boldly patterned curtains – repainting the walls periodically will update the room.

· Think about proportions. Large floral or geometric designs look great on curtains for big windows, such as romantic floor-length drapes for a bedroom or a bold treatment for patio doors. Small prints work best on curtains for smaller windows like those in a bathroom or box room.

· If there is a good view from your window make it a focal point by having bold, bright curtains. If the window isn't overlooked you could dress it with pretty patterned voile, which will still let in lots of light.

TOOLS AND EQUIPMENT

✓ Basic sewing kit (see p. 8)

SMALL, SCATTERED FLOWERS ARE PARTICULARLY SUITED TO SMALL WINDOWS.

LEAF SHAPES ARE TIMELESS AND CAN RANGE FROM ALL-OVER PATTERNS TO LARGE INDIVIDUAL MOTIFS.

STRIPES MAKE A BOLD STATEMENT. VERTICAL STRIPES WILL ADD HEIGHT AND HORIZONTAL ONES WILL WIDEN A WINDOW.

YOU CAN PICK OUT ACCENT COLOURS IN OTHER FURNISHINGS WITH SPOT-PRINTED FABRIC.

ALLOWING FOR THE PATTERN REPEAT

When making curtains in pairs or those that need more than one drop to make up the width, it is important to match the pattern across the whole width. To achieve this, you need to make an allowance for the pattern repeat in your calculations to make sure you buy enough fabric, and you also need to take it into consideration when cutting the lengths.

The term 'pattern repeat' is used to describe the depth of the pattern that repeats down the length of the fabric and is expressed as a measurement. It is often easiest to measure from the top of a dominant motif down through the pattern, including any plain fabric between the motifs, to the top of the same motif the next time it occurs directly under the first.

SEWING SENSE

The pattern repeat is usually given on the fabric bolt or on the back of a sample. If you are not sure, ask the store assistant to confirm the measurement for you.

FIGURE 1
TO FIND THE PATTERN REPEAT, MEASURE FROM THE TOP OF ONE MOTIF TO THE TOP OF THE SAME MOTIF DIRECTLY BELOW.

One pattern repeat

Bold patterns look good in the bottom third of the curtain

POSITIONING THE DOMINANT PATTERN

If the fabric you have chosen has a very striking pattern and you have plenty of fabric, it is a good idea to decide where you want the most dominant motifs to fall, because they catch the eye most easily. For example, if the fabric has an evenly distributed pattern, you could plan to have the top of one of the main motifs running along the top of the header so the pattern doesn't

FIGURE
THE REPEAT ON AN UNEVEN STRIPE OR SMALL PRINT MIGHT BE 2—4IN (5—10CM). ON A LARGE FLORAL DESIGN, IT MIGHT BE AS MUCH AS 27½IN (70CM).

appear to end abruptly. Alternatively, if the fabric has some areas of pattern that are denser than others, it looks best to have the boldest pattern a third of the way from the top or bottom of the curtain so that the pattern doesn't look top-heavy.

CALCULATING THE EXTRA REQUIREMENTS

Having determined the basic drop for the window to be dressed (see p. 30), you need to add the pattern repeat, as well as the regular allowances, to each drop before calculating the total length of fabric needed. To continue with the second example on p. 31, if the basic drop is 69in (175cm) and the pattern repeat is 16in (41cm), you will need 85in (216cm) for every drop. Finish your calculations for the total length of fabric required as explained on p. 31.

MATCHING THE PATTERN

1 If necessary, square the top edge of the fabric (see p. 29). With the right side uppermost, cut the first panel to the measurement of the basic drop (i.e. including allowances for the header and hem, but not including the pattern repeat). Remember to take the positioning of the pattern into account if that is important.

2 Keeping the first panel in position, unroll another length of fabric alongside it, matching the pattern at the side edges so that the pattern continues across. This will probably mean that there is some fabric above as well as below the length of the first panel. Alternatively, if you have less space to work in, place the first panel face down over the remaining fabric, matching the pattern. Check that the pattern matches down the length of both panels.

Excess from pattern repeat allowance

Basic drop + hem and header allowances

FIGURE 3 MAKE SURE THE PATTERN MATCHES ON BOTH PIECES OF FABRIC BEFORE CUTTING THE SECOND PANEL.

3 Cut the second panel across the top and bottom, using the first panel as a guide. Continue matching and cutting until you have the correct number of panels.

SEWING SENSE

If each curtain is to be made of more than one panel, stitch the panels together from the hem edge to the top. That way, if the pattern repeat goes out of alignment, any discrepancy will be in the folds at the top and thus less visible.

CUTTING HALF PANELS

You may need a half- or even quarter-width panel to make up the total width of a curtain. To do this accurately, measure from one side edge to the centre or quarter mark at intervals down the length of the fabric. Draw a chalk line through the marks and then cut the panel.

FIGURE 4
CUT THE HALF-WIDTH PANEL ACCURATELY SO THAT THE PATTERN MATCHES DOWN THE OUTER EDGE OF THE MAIN PANEL.

Main panel for the inside edge of the curtain

Half panel for the outside edge of the curtain

Always use part panels down the outer edges of the curtain so that when the curtains are drawn, complete panels will meet in the middle and the joins will be less obvious.

FIGURE 5 POSITION THE HALF PANEL ON THE SIDE EDGE. THE COMPLETE ONE IN THE CENTRE.

SEWING SENSE

While you are cutting the main fabric it makes sense to also cut out the lining. Cut the same number of lining panels as the main fabric, but to the basic drop (i.e. not including the pattern repeat).

gorgeous GOBLET CURTAINS

THIS STYLISH CURTAIN WAS MADE FROM ONE WIDTH OF FABRIC, WHICH FEATURES A FRESH AND PRETTY LEAF PATTERN. IF YOU NEED WIDER CURTAINS, OR MORE THAN ONE, PATTERNED FABRIC WILL NEED TO BE MATCHED, AND THESE INSTRUCTIONS CAN BE ADAPTED TO HOWEVER MANY PANELS OF FABRIC YOU NEED. THE FABRIC CHOSEN HERE HAS A RELATIVELY SMALL PATTERN REPEAT, MAKING IT ECONOMICAL TO USE.

CLASSIC GOBLET PLEATS ARE VERY ELEGANT AND PARTICULARLY SUITABLE FOR FULL-LENGTH CURTAINS. THE LOOK IS EASY TO ACHIEVE USING SPECIAL HEADER TAPE, WHICH MAKES SURE THE FABRIC IS EVENLY PLEATED ACROSS THE TOP AND CASCADES IN SOFT FOLDS DOWN TO THE GROUND.

FABRIC CALCULATION

1 Measure the curtain drop (see p. 30). Then add:
- 8in (20cm) for the hem
- double the depth of the goblet header tape, plus ¼in (6mm)
- the pattern repeat (see p. 104).

2 Measure the basic width across the window (see p. 30). Then:
- double the measurement for fullness
- add an allowance for seams and side hems (see p. 30)
  If you prefer to keep things simple, you can just add an allowance of 4in (10cm) for all seams and side hems in this project.

3 Work out how many widths of fabric you need. Then multiply the total drop by the number of widths to give you the total length of fabric (see also pp. 30–31).

YOU WILL NEED

- ✓ Curtain fabric (as calculated above)
- ✓ Lining fabric (as for curtain fabric, minus pattern repeat allowance)
- ✓ Goblet header tape (add ½yd (50cm) to total width of each curtain)
- ✓ 2–3 reels of general-purpose sewing thread per curtain
- ✓ Basic sewing kit (see p. 8)

TECHNICAL KNOW-HOW
Calculating fabric requirements (see pp. 30–31)
Working with patterned fabric (pp. 104–105)
Using header tape (pp. 92–97)

MAKING GOBLET-PLEATED CURTAINS

MAKING THE MAIN PANELS

1 With the right side uppermost, cut the first panel of curtain fabric, including the hem and header allowances but not the pattern repeat. Take the positioning of the pattern into consideration if you wish and have sufficient fabric. Cut the remaining panels, matching the pattern as necessary (see p. 105).

2 Cut the same number of panels for the lining to the length of the first panel of curtain fabric without the pattern repeat. Leave to one side.

3 Pin the curtain fabric panels together, matching the pattern, to make the total width for each curtain. Sew any seams needed, using regular straight seams and machine sewing from hem to top. Neaten the seam allowances with overcast or zigzag stitch (see p. 18). Press the seams.

4 Turn the raw edges under by $3/8$in (1cm) down both side edges. Turn the side edges under again by the same amount to make $3/4$in (2cm) double hems. Press in place. Turn up the bottom hem allowance to make a double hem of 4in (10cm). Press and pin the hem. Do not stitch any of the hems.

5 Turn down the top edge by the depth of the header tape plus $1/8$in (3mm). Then turn the same amount again. Pin the header allowance in place. Check the finished length of the curtain by measuring from the hem to the top edge. Refold the top edge to correct any inaccuracy. Press and pin in place. Do not stitch, but set the fabric to one side.

MAKING THE LINING

1 Piece the lining together in the same manner as the main fabric. There is no need to turn side hems.

2 Turn up the hem allowance to make a double hem of 4in (10cm). Press and machine stitch the hem in place.

ATTACHING THE LINING

1 Lay the curtain panel right side down, temporarily opening out the hems. Place the lining wrong side down over the curtain so the seam edges align and the bottom of the lining hem is about 2in (5cm) above the bottom of the curtain hem.

2 Pin through the lining and curtain fabric at the hem. Then, working from the bottom and up through the centre line, smooth the lining in place and pin it at intervals to hold the layers together.

EXPERT TIP

YOU COULD USE LARGE SAFETY PINS, WHICH WON'T SLIP OUT, TO SECURE THE LINING TO THE CURTAIN FABRIC.

3 If necessary, trim the top of the lining so it is in line with the top edge of the curtain. Then refold the header allowance, tuck the lining under the allowance and re-pin.

Lining RS

FIGURE 1
RE-PIN THE HEADER ALLOWANCE AFTER POSITIONING THE LINING.

Fold

Bottom edge of the hemmed curtain — Hem allowance

4 Repeat step 3 for the side edges, trimming the lining so it matches the side edges of the finished curtain. Refold the side hems, tuck under the raw edge of the lining and re-pin.

5 Finish the side edges either by hand stitching the curtain fabric to the lining (see pp. 15–16) or by top stitching on the machine (see p.19), starting 5in (13cm) up from the bottom hem.

ATTACHING THE HEADER TAPE

1 Find the centre of the header tape along its length. With the loops on the tape uppermost, insert a pin downwards through the centre of the goblet section nearest the centre point of the tape. Use another pin to mark the centre of the flat area between goblets nearest the centre point of the tape. Finally mark the centre of the curtain panel at the top of the header allowance.

FIGURE 2 FIND THE CENTRE OF THE CENTRAL GOBLET AND FLAT SECTIONS ON THE HEADER TAPE.

EXPERT TIP
MANY HEADER TAPES HAVE A COLOURED LINE TO INDICATE THE BOTTOM OF THE TAPE.

2 Line up each of the pins on the header tape with the one on the curtain to see which one leaves the most flat tape (i.e. not a goblet) at the outside edges of the curtain. Choose the best match and pin the tape to the curtain.

FIGURE 3
MATCH THE PINS THAT ALLOW FOR A FLAT SECTION OF TAPE AT EACH SIDE OF THE CURTAIN.

WS

EXPERT TIP
THE FINISHED CURTAIN WILL HANG BETTER IF THERE IS A FLAT PIECE OF TAPE, RATHER THAN A GOBLET, AT EACH SIDE EDGE.

3 Pin the top edge of the tape in place a scant ⅛in (3mm) down from the top of the curtain. Place the pins two finger widths from the edge, so you can machine stitch without moving or hitting the pins. Pin the other long edge in the same way without trimming the ends. Decide which side edge of the curtain will be the leading edge and machine stitch through the tape only, to secure the cords at that end. Trim the tape to about 1¼in (3cm) beyond the width of the curtain and then tuck the raw ends under so that the tape comes to about ¼in (6mm) from the edge of the fabric. Pin the ends.

EXPERT TIP
SEW ACROSS ONE END OF THE TAPE TO SECURE THE CORDS SO THAT THEY WILL NOT PULL WHEN GATHERING THE HEADER FROM THE OTHER END.

4 Using the machine, straight stitch the tape in place close to the edges. Start at the bottom left corner, continuing up the side, along the top edge and down the opposite side to the bottom right, keeping the cords out of the way. Secure and cut the threads. Start stitching again at the bottom left, but this time machine along the bottom of the tape.

Start stitching here

FIGURE 4 ATTACH THE HEADER TAPE ALONG THE SIDE AND TOP EDGES FIRST, BEFORE STITCHING ALONG THE BOTTOM EDGE IN THE SAME DIRECTION TO THE TOP.

EXPERT TIP
MACHINING THE TOP AND BOTTOM OF THE HEADER TAPE IN THE SAME DIRECTION STOPS IT TWISTING.

FORMING THE GOBLET PLEATS

1 To gather the pleats, pull the top cord in the header from the outer edge of the curtain and push the top of the first goblet into position. Then pull the bottom cord so the first two pleats meet to form the stem below the goblet. Push the finished goblet along and form the next one in the same way. Repeat, until the whole curtain is pleated with goblets. Tie a slipknot in the cords to hold them securely and keep the goblets in place.

2 Secure the goblets on the front of the curtain, overstitching together the two pleats that form the stem just below the tape. You could add buttons, braid or beads to hide the stitching and add decorative detail. You could also fill each goblet cup with wadding to pad them out so that they hold their shape.

HEMMING THE CURTAINS

1 Unpin the curtain hems and hang the curtains for 24 hours before hemming.

2 Check the length is still even across the curtains, adjusting the hem if necessary. Neaten at each end of the hem by mitring the corners (see p. 45) or by trimming the excess fabric and tucking the hem allowance under the side hems. Re-pin and then hand stitch the hem using blind stitch (see p. 15).

MAKING SWAGS AND JABOTS

SWAGS AND JABOTS MAKE A FORMAL WINDOW DRESSING. THEY WORK WELL ON THEIR OWN OR CAN BE TEAMED WITH FULL-LENGTH CURTAINS FOR A MORE LUXURIOUS LOOK. THEY CAN BE DRAPED OVER A POLE, STAPLED TO A FIXED BATTEN (DESCRIBED HERE) OR ATTACHED WITH HOOK AND LOOP TAPE TO A POLE (SEE PP. 116—119) OR BATTEN.

THE METHOD GIVEN HERE FOR MAKING THE SWAGS AND JABOTS CAN BE USED TO PRODUCE AS MANY SWAGS AS YOU NEED AND EVEN A CENTRAL JABOT. CHANGE THE LOOK BY ADDING A TRIM, FRINGE OR, AS ON PP. 116—119, USING FABRICS IN COMPLEMENTARY COLOURS.

TOOLS AND EQUIPMENT
✓ Basic sewing kit (see p. 8)
✓ Calico or sheeting to make pattern
✓ Ironing board

SWAGS

'Swag' is the term for the draped or pleated folds of fabric that extend across the top of the window. Although they may look difficult to achieve, you can soon learn the tricks of the trade to get them hanging perfectly. The number of swags is determined by the width of the window. It is usually more visually pleasing to work in odd numbers, using one, three or five swags across a window.

The part of the swag on view should be no more than 40in (100cm) wide. The width can be altered by increasing or decreasing the overlap of adjoining swags. Allow 4–5in (10–13cm) for overlapping, which is usually enough to ensure that the top of the window is covered. The depth of the swags should be in proportion to the width, so allow for them to be approximately one-sixth of the height of the window and no more than 20in (50cm).

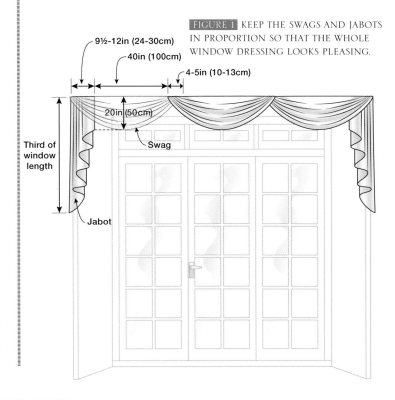

FIGURE 1 KEEP THE SWAGS AND JABOTS IN PROPORTION SO THAT THE WHOLE WINDOW DRESSING LOOKS PLEASING.

9½-12in (24-30cm)
40in (100cm)
4-5in (10-13cm)
20in (50cm)
Third of window length
Swag
Jabot

JABOTS

Jabots are gathered or softly pleated side panels that accompany swags. They usually have an asymmetric hem. They can be part of the same piece of fabric as the swags or can be made and fixed separately. Jabots are also known as 'tails' and 'cascades'.

The length of the jabots should be about one-third of the window height, with the shortest fold falling to the same level as the bottom of the swags. The finished width of a jabot is usually about 9½–12in (24–30cm) wide.

SEWING SENSE

Swags and jabots should always be lined, as the reverse side will show. Choose a fabric that complements the main fabric.

CALCULATING FABRIC REQUIREMENTS

1 To calculate the amount of fabric required for each swag, first drape a tape measure across the top of the window or from the curtain pole to simulate the swag shape. If the tape measurement, plus 2in (5cm), is less than the width of the fabric, you will need 1yd (1m) per swag. If that measurement is wider than the fabric, allow 2yd (2m) per swag. Note the finished width of the swag along the pole. Determine how many swags will fit along the pole, allowing them to overlap by 4–5in (10–13cm).

Finished width of swag

Add 2in (5cm) for fabric width

FIGURE 2 SIMULATE THE SWAG AND TAKE MEASUREMENTS.

2 For each jabot, you will need a full width of fabric. If the jabot is to be fixed to a batten and therefore has a return around the side of the batten, make sure you have enough fabric for this too. Allow for the length of each jabot, adding 1in (2.5cm) for the seam allowances on each one. Window dressings usually have two jabots.

3 You will need the same amount of lining as the main fabric.

MAKING A TEST SWAG

This step is crucial if you want your swags to drape perfectly. Use a piece of calico or an old sheet so you can use the cut shape as the pattern for the actual swag.

1 Cut a piece of fabric 36in (90cm) long with a width the same as the tape measurement plus 32in (75cm) for adjustments. Fold the fabric in half lengthways and mark the centre point at the top and bottom.

2 At the top of the fabric, mark the finished width of the swag, centring the previous mark. At the bottom of the fabric, mark the tape measurement, again centring the previous mark. Join the ends of the lines together to form two diagonal lines. Decide on the number of folds required (have more folds for deeper swags, fewer for shallower ones). Then mark the folds at equal distances along the diagonal lines, allowing for one more space than the number of folds.

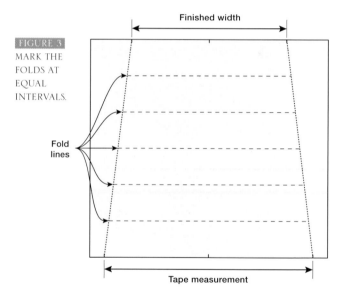

Finished width

FIGURE 3 MARK THE FOLDS AT EQUAL INTERVALS.

Fold lines

Tape measurement

3 Pin the top edge of the fabric to the edge of an ironing board or the back of the sofa. Fold up and pin the first marks on the diagonal lines. Continue to pin and drape the folds, starting at alternate sides each time. Adjust the folds as necessary.

FIGURE 4 PIN ALL THE FOLDS IN PLACE.

4 Mark a cutting line on the fold that was pinned up last, 1in (2.5cm) from the outer edges and approximately 3in (7.5cm) up from the bottom edge. Trim the excess fabric in a continuous sweep along the cutting line.

FIGURE 5 NEATLY TRIM THE SIDE AND BOTTOM EDGES OF THE TOP LAYER OF FABRIC.

5 Unpin the trimmed fold and pin it out of the way. Measure and mark a cutting line down across the remaining pleats about 1½in (4cm) outside the finished width on each side of the swag. Trim the excess fabric, cutting through all the remaining layers.

FIGURE 6 TRIM VERTICALLY THROUGH ALL THE UNDERLYING LAYERS.

Cut

SEWING SENSE

Buy the best fabric that your budget will allow and pre-launder before cutting to ensure that any shrinkage happens before the fabric is made up.

6 Unpin the swag and press. Fold the fabric in half lengthways to check that the folds are balanced both sides. Trim them to match if necessary.

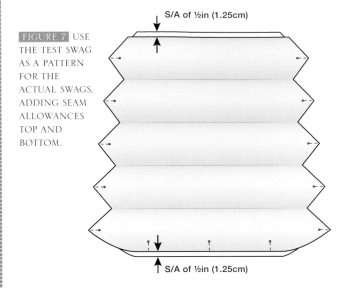

FIGURE 7 USE THE TEST SWAG AS A PATTERN FOR THE ACTUAL SWAGS. ADDING SEAM ALLOWANCES TOP AND BOTTOM.

S/A of ½in (1.25cm)

S/A of ½in (1.25cm)

MAKING SWAGS

Your test swag now makes the perfect pattern for cutting out the actual swags.

1 Using the test swag as a pattern and adding seam allowances of ½in (1.25cm) to the top and bottom edges, cut out the main fabric and the lining for each swag.

2 Sew the lining to the main fabric, right sides together, along the bottom edge. Trim the seam allowance, turn right sides out and press. Zigzag stitch or overlock the side and upper edges of fabric and lining together.

3 Fold and pin the swag to the ironing board as before, adjusting the pleats. Baste and then machine stitch through all the layers to hold the pleats in place.

EXPERT TIP

IF YOUR FABRIC HAS A PATTERN, MAKE SURE YOU CUT THE FABRIC SO THAT THE PATTERN ON THE SWAGS AND JABOTS MATCHES ACROSS THE WINDOW.

MAKING JABOTS

These jabots have a return so that they look smart at the ends of a batten or a track with returns. If you don't need a return, just take off the extra allowance.

1 Mark out the shape of the jabot on the fabric. The width should be three times the width of the finished jabot to allow for pleating, plus the width of the return. Add two ½in (1.25cm) side seams.

Finished width x 3 plus return plus 1in (2.5cm)

FIGURE 8 MARK OUT THE JABOT ON THE FABRIC.

Swag drop (or longer) plus 1in (2.5cm)

Outside drop plus 1in (2.5cm)

Return 2in–4in (5cm–10cm)

2 The inside drop should be the same length as the depth of the swag. The outside drop can be one- or two-thirds of the curtain drop to the sill or the floor. Add ½in (1.25cm) seam allowances along the top and bottom edges.

3 Cut one jabot from the main fabric and lining. Reverse the pattern and cut another piece of main fabric and lining for the second jabot.

4 Trim ½in (1.25cm) from the diagonal edge of the main fabric. With right sides facing and matching the raw edges, pin the main fabric to the lining along the diagonal edge only. Sew a ½in (1.25cm) seam. Trim the seam and press it towards the lining. Turn through.

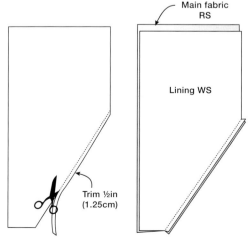

FIGURE 9 TRIM THE LINING SO IT IS SLIGHTLY SHORTER THAN THE MAIN FABRIC.

Main fabric RS

Lining WS

Trim ½in (1.25cm)

5 Working on a flat surface with the lining uppermost, pin the raw edges together, rolling the diagonal seam towards the lining so a little of the main fabric is visible. Sew ½in (1.25cm) side seams. Trim the bottom corner and turn right sides out. Press.

FIGURE 10 STITCH THE SIDE SEAMS AND TRIM THE BOTTOM CORNERS.

Lining WS

Roll

Press seam allowances towards lining

6 Gather or pleat the top edge as desired and baste to hold it in place.

HANGING SWAGS AND JABOTS

Swags and jabots can be hung in a number of different ways. Here, the method for attaching them to a batten is described, but they can also be attached to a pole using hook and loop tape as shown on p. 119.

1 Press a turning allowance along the top edge of all the swags and jabots. Mount the swags first, following your plan as to which ones should overlap others. Staple each one to the top of the batten, aligning the top fold along the top front edge. Arrange the pleats neatly.

2 Attach the jabots in the same way at each end of the batten, folding the fabric around the batten ends to make a neat return.

SEWING SENSE
Avoid seams twisting or buckling by stitching them all in the same direction. Press each seam before stitching over it again.

a different view of

SWAGS
AND JABOTS

THIS IS THE PERFECT WINDOW
DRESSING FOR A WINDOW THAT ISN'T
OVERLOOKED. THE METHODS FOR
MAKING THE SWAGS AND JABOTS ARE
VERY SIMILAR TO THOSE ON PP. 112–115.
HOWEVER, THEY ARE HUNG FROM A
CURTAIN POLE, INSTEAD OF A BATTEN,
USING HOOK AND LOOP TAPE, WHICH
IS QUICK AND EASY TO USE. THE SWAGS
ALSO FEATURE A CONTRAST BINDING
ALONG THE BOTTOM EDGES, WHICH
MAKES THEM LOOK VERY SMART.

FABRIC CALCULATION

1 Determine how many swags will fit along the pole, allowing them to overlap by 4–5in (10–13cm). Calculate the amount of main fabric and the contrast fabric (lining) following the guidance on p. 113, and allowing for any pattern repeat (see p. 104).

2 For the jabots, follow the advice on p. 113, and also allow for any pattern repeat (see p. 104).

YOU WILL NEED

- ✓ Main fabric (as calculated above)
- ✓ Contrast fabric (as main fabric)
- ✓ Matching/contrasting bias binding
- ✓ Hook and loop tape
- ✓ Basic sewing kit (see p. 8)

TECHNICAL KNOW-HOW

Matching pattern repeats (p. 105)
Making swags and jabots (pp. 112–115)

MAKING THE SWAGS

1 Follow the technique on pp. 113–114 to make a test swag and a fabric pattern. Using the pattern, cut the swag on the bias of the main fabric, adding seam allowances. Repeat for the contrast fabric.

EXPERT TIP

CUT THESE SWAGS OUT ON THE BIAS SO THAT THEY HANG GRACEFULLY. THE BIAS IS FOUND AT A 45-DEGREE ANGLE TO THE SELVAGES.

2 With right sides together, stitch the main fabric to the contrast fabric along the top edge. Clip the seam, turn rights side out and press. Baste the bottom curved raw edges together. Overlock the side edges to neaten them.

3 Stitch bias binding to the bottom edge of the swag to neaten the raw edges. Fold the binding over the raw edges and top stitch it in place. Alternatively, open out the binding and stitch it to the fabric, right sides together with the main fabric and raw edges matching. Then trim the seam, turn the binding towards the contrast fabric and slip stitch it in place. Press.

FIGURE 1 ATTACH THE BIAS BINDING TO THE BOTTOM EDGES OF THE SWAGS.

4 Pin and stitch the pleats of the swag in place as explained in step 3 on p. 114. Stitch a length of loop tape on the reverse side close to the top edge of the swag. Make the rest of the swags in the same way.

MAKING THE JABOTS

1 Mark out the shape of the jabot on the fabric. The width should be three times the width of the finished jabot to allow for pleating. The inside drop should be the depth of the swag; the outside drop as long as you wish. Add ½in (1.25cm) seam allowances all around.

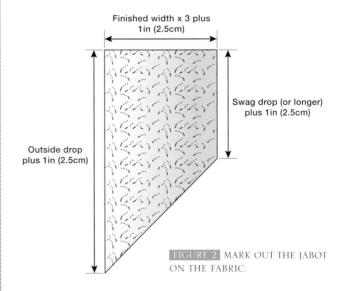

FIGURE 2 MARK OUT THE JABOT ON THE FABRIC.

2 Cut one jabot from the main fabric and lining. Reverse the pattern and cut another piece of main fabric and lining for the second jabot.

3 With the right sides of one fabric and one lining together, stitch the two sides and the diagonal bottom edge. Trim the corners, turn through and press. Repeat this process for the other pair of fabrics.

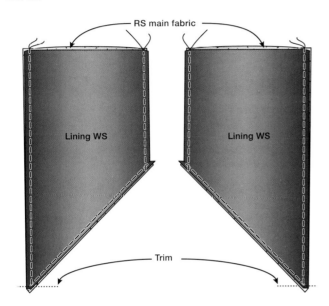

FIGURE 3 TRIM ACROSS THE CORNERS SO THAT, WHEN YOU TURN THE JABOTS THROUGH, THE CORNERS LOOK VERY SHARP AND PROFESSIONAL.

SEWING SENSE

Always baste in a contrasting colour so that it is easy to remove the stitching later.

4 Measure the top edge of the jabot and mark eight fold lines at equal intervals. Fold the jabot into pleats, concertina fashion. Overlock or zigzag stitch the top raw edges to neaten them and hold the pleats together. Stitch a length of loop tape on the reverse side close to the top edge of the jabot. Finish the second jabot as a mirror image of the first.

FIGURE 4 PLEAT THE JABOT CONCERTINA FASHION.

HANGING THE SWAGS AND JABOTS

1 Mark where the swags and jabots go on the pole. Then wrap self-adhesive hook tape around the pole at these points in candy-cane fashion.

FIGURE 5 WRAP HOOK TAPE SECURELY AROUND THE POLE.

2 Mount the swags first, taking the top edges of each swag to the back of the pole and ensuring that the hook and loop tapes hold them securely. Arrange the pleats neatly.

3 Add the jabots at each end of the pole, taking them as far round the back as necessary for the loop tape to grip the hook tape. Make sure both jabots hang to the same length on the inside and outside edges.

MAKING VALANCES

A VALANCE IS A SOFT FABRIC HEADING THAT HANGS DOWN OVER THE TOP EDGE OF CURTAINS AS PART OF A WINDOW TREATMENT OR SOFTENS THE TOP EDGES OF A BLIND OR AN OTHERWISE BARE WINDOW. VALANCES CAN BE GATHERED ALONG A CASING ONTO A POLE, HUNG FROM A HEADER TAPE JUST LIKE CURTAINS OR TWISTED AND FOLDED AROUND A POLE. THE BOTTOM HEM CAN BE STRAIGHT OR SHAPED AND THE LINING SHOULD BE COORDINATED WELL BECAUSE IT WILL BE ON SHOW THROUGH THE WINDOW.

TOOLS AND EQUIPMENT

✓ Basic sewing kit (see p. 8)
✓ Valance pole or track

VALANCE CHOICES

- You could line the valance with the main fabric – just double the quantity of fabric.
- Trim the bottom edge of the valance with a coordinating or contrasting trim such as fringing or beading.
- Add decorative details to the valance header in the form of buttons, rosettes or a plaited fabric rope.

INSTALLATION

Most valances are hung from a pole or track fixed just above the window frame. If the valance is part of a layered window treatment, consider a double track, which only requires one set of fixings. To hang a valance from a track, make it as you would a curtain, attaching the desired header tape (see pp. 92–95).

If you use two separate poles, ensure there is a minimum of 2in (5cm) between them and that the valance pole extends beyond the curtain pole at each end. A casing allows a valance to be fed easily along a pole and the method for making one is given opposite.

SEWING SENSE

A pelmet is similar to a valance and is, also, fixed to the top of the window. However, a pelmet is usually fixed to a wooden batten and provides a solid flat surface that can be covered with fabric or painted).

CALCULATING FABRIC REQUIREMENTS

1 Measure the drop of the valance from the top of the pole or track to the required length. A length of one-third of the window height often works well. Then add:

- 1in (2.5cm) for seams
- 1in (2.5cm) for ease
- the pattern repeat (see p.104) if necessary.

2 Measure the finished width of the valance from one end of the pole or track to the other, including around the returns and then:

- multiply the measurement by 1½, 2 or 2½ for fullness
- add allowances for seams and side hems.

3 Work out how many widths of fabric you need. Then multiply the total drop by the number of widths to give you the total length of fabric. You will need the same amount of lining, minus any allowance for a pattern repeat.

MAKING A VALANCE WITH A CASING

This type of valance looks lovely in soft gathers along a curtain pole or rod.

1 Cut the fabric panels for the main valance and the lining.

EXPERT TIP

IF YOU NEED TO USE PART OF A PANEL TO MAKE UP THE TOTAL WIDTH, CUT THE PART PANEL IN HALF LENGTHWAYS AND USE THE TWO PIECES ON THE OUTER EDGES OF THE VALANCE TO MINIMIZE THE NUMBER OF SEAMS ACROSS THE CENTRE OF IT.

2 Sew all the fabric panels for the valance together. Neaten the seams and press them to one side, in the same direction. Piece the lining together in the same way.

EXPERT TIP

PRESSING THE SEAMS IN THE SAME DIRECTION ALLOWS THE CURTAIN POLE TO RUN MORE SMOOTHLY THROUGH THE CASING.

3 Place the main fabric and lining on a flat surface, right sides together. Mark the position for the casing at the side edges, allowing for the depth of the pole plus 1in (2.5cm) for the seam and ease allowance.

4 Machine stitch around the outer edges, taking a ⅜in (1cm) seam allowance and leaving an opening for turning in addition to openings for the pole pocket. Press and trim across the corners.

Pole diameter + 1in (2.5cm)

Turning opening

FIGURE 1 STITCH THE LINING TO THE MAIN FABRIC, LEAVING OPENINGS FOR TURNING AND THE POLE.

5 Turn the valance right sides out and press again, tucking the raw edges of the openings inside. Slip stitch the turning opening closed.

6 Mark the bottom of the pole pocket across the top of the valance. Stitch through all the layers.

FIGURE 2 STITCH ACROSS TO FORM THE POLE POCKET.

7 Feed the pole through the casing and gather the valance evenly across the width.

RUFFLED CASING

To create a small ruffle at the top of the casing you will need to follow the steps for Making a valance with a casing (left), allowing an additional 1½in (4cm) to the length. Then, at step 3, mark the position for the casing 1½in (4cm) below the top edge. Stitch as instructed in step 4 and turn through. Mark the lower edge of the casing horizontally and stitch. Mark another horizontal line above the pole depth plus 3cm for ease and, again, top stitch through all thicknesses.

TRIMMING A VALANCE

1 If you wish to add a trim or ruffle along the bottom edge of the valance, deduct the depth of it from the total length of the valance as part of your fabric calculations.

FIGURE 3 DEDUCT THE DEPTH OF THE TRIM WHEN YOU CALCULATE HOW MUCH FABRIC YOU NEED.

2 Pin the top edge of the trim or ruffle to the right side of the lower edge of the valance and machine stitch it in place. Then add the lining, sandwiching the trim between the layers. Once stitched and turned right sides out, the trim will hang down.

FIGURE 4 THE TRIM HANGS FREELY BELOW THE FINISHED VALANCE.

CREATING A PUFFED VALANCE

To achieve the puffed effect, make up a basic valance and turn it right sides out. Then stuff it with fibrefill or soft tissue paper before slip stitching the turning opening closed.

FIGURE 5 STUFF THE BOTTOM OF A VALANCE TO GIVE IT A PUFFED APPEARANCE.

CREATING A TWISTED VALANCE

This is a fun finish for windows with straight curtain panels or blinds. Use two crisp complementary fabrics such as cotton chintz. Stitch the pole pocket across the centre of the valance panel. Feed the valance onto the pole and then twist it around at even intervals so that both fabrics show alternately.

A SOFT VALANCE IS THE PERFECT TOPPER TO SOFTEN THE HARD EDGES OF THE WINDOW FRAME.

FIGURE 6 TWIST THE VALANCE SO THAT BOTH FABRICS SHOW.

ruffled and
TAPERED VALANCE

THIS SOFTLY SHAPED VALANCE IS FED
ALONG A POLE WITH RETURNS SO THAT
IT STANDS AWAY FROM THE WINDOW
FRAME. IT HAS A RUFFLED HEAD WITH
SWEEPING TAILS DOWN THE SIDES. YOU
COULD ADAPT THE METHOD ON P. 127,
GATHERING THE TAILS MORE FULLY SO
THAT THEY CASCADE DOWN IN FOLDS.
THE HEM OF THIS TREATMENT COULD
BE DECORATED WITH A CONTRASTING
BINDING, RUFFLE OR BOUGHT TRIM.

FABRIC CALCULATIONS

1 Measure the drop of the valance from the top of the pole or track to the required length on the outside edges. The valance in the photograph sits just below sill length. Then add:

- 1in (2.5cm) for seams
- 1in (2.5cm) for ease
- 3in (7.5cm) for ruffle
- the pattern repeat (see p.104) if necessary.

2 Measure the finished width of the valance from one end of the track to the other, including around the returns and then:

- double the measurement for fullness
- add allowances for seams and side hems.

3 Work out how many widths of fabric you need. Then multiply the total drop by the number of widths to give you the total length of fabric. You will need the same amount of lining, minus any allowance for a pattern repeat.

YOU WILL NEED

✓ Main fabric (as calculated above)
✓ Lining (as main fabric)
✓ 2–3 reels of general-purpose sewing thread

TECHNIQUES USED
Making a valance casing (see p. 121)

MAKING THE VALANCE

1 Cut and sew together the main fabric panels to make up the total width. Press the seams open. Make up the lining in the same way.

2 Fold the main fabric in half lengthways and place it on a flat surface. Mark the shape of the valance, remembering that you are working on half of it and allowing for the double fullness. On the folded edge, mark the length of the valance in the centre, allowing for the pole diameter plus 1in (2.5cm) for ease, 3in (7.5cm) for the ruffle and ³⁄₈in (1cm) for each of two seams.

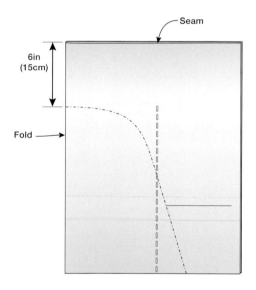

FIGURE 1 MARK THE BASIC SHAPE OF THE VALANCE ON THE FOLDED FABRIC.

3 On the outside edge, mark the longest length of the valance, adding the same allowances as in step 2.

4 Decide how far you want the shortest part of the valance to run before dropping down into the tails. As a rough guide, it should extent for about a third of the total width of the fabric. Mark a line for the extent of the short part and then continue to make a smooth curve and drop down to the longest point.

5 Cut along this line through both layers. Then use the main fabric as a pattern to cut the lining to the same shape.

6 With right sides together, stitch the lining and main fabric all around the edges, leaving an opening to turn through and the two openings for the pole 3in (7.5cm) down from the top seam.

FIGURE 2 STITCH AROUND THE EDGES, LEAVING OPENINGS FOR THE POLE AND FOR TURNING.

7 Trim the seams and clip into the curves. Turn the valance right sides out and press. Slip stitch the turning opening closed.

8 Mark two parallel stitch lines for the casing, one 3in (7.5cm) from the top edge, the other the diameter of the pole plus 1in (2.5cm) from the first. Stitch along the lines to form the casing.

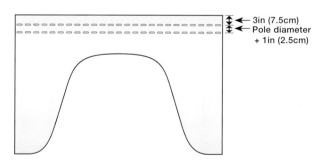

FIGURE 3 STITCH THE CASING, ALLOWING FOR THE RUFFLE ABOVE.

9 Insert the pole into the casing and gather the fabric fullness evenly. Fix the pole to the brackets on the wall.

MAKING LININGS AND INTERLININGS

LININGS ARE SEEN ON THE REVERSE SIDE OF CURTAINS, THROUGH THE WINDOW OR SOMETIMES WHEN A CURTAIN IS DRAWN BACK INTO A TIEBACK OR A JABOT IS FOLDED TO DECORATIVE EFFECT. THEY NEATEN THE BACK OF THE MAIN FABRIC, HIDING THE SEAMS, PROTECT THE MAIN FABRIC FROM SUN DAMAGE AND HELP KEEP HEAT IN AND LIGHT AND NOISE OUT.

A LINING GIVES A CURTAIN WEIGHT AND BODY, AND AN INTERLINING PROVIDES A THIRD LAYER TO ADD TO THIS EFFECT. AN INTERLINING CANNOT BE SEEN, BUT IT ENHANCES THE FULLNESS OF THE CURTAIN AND GIVES A RICHER EFFECT — FOLDS APPEAR DEEPER AND SOFTER.

TOOLS AND EQUIPMENT
✓ Basic sewing kit (see p. 8)

LINING CHOICES

- Linings and interlinings are usually made of fabric of a similar or lighter weight to the main curtain fabric. It is best to choose a pale or complementary colour if you want to avoid the colour showing through a pale-coloured curtain.
- Linings are traditionally made from white or off-white cotton sateen – they don't affect the colour or pattern of the main fabric and the shiny sateen finish helps to repel dust.
- Consider a coloured or even a printed lining if the reverse of the window treatment is going to be visible or you want the curtains to be double-sided to ring the changes.
- Consider lining all your windows facing the same direction with the same colour to create a uniform look.
- Use fabric with a smooth weave for interlining, such as cotton, unbleached muslin or even sheeting.

SEWING SENSE
Interlining is particularly suitable for glamorous fabrics such as velvet and silk, and long length curtains, as shown in the unadulterated luxury of the feather-trimmed curtains on pp. 134–139.

CALCULATING LINING FABRIC REQUIREMENTS

Linings can be sewn into the construction of the curtain or be completely separate. A loose lining is attached from hooks and special header tape to the reverse of the main curtain after it has been gathered. A sew-in lining needs to be the same width as the curtain, whereas loose linings can be less full.

A sew-in lining needs to be the same size as the main curtain panel, although, if the lining is plain, you do not need to make any allowance for pattern. When working out how many drops you need to make up the total width of the lining, remember that your lining fabric may be a different width to the main fabric.

EXPERT TIP

CHOOSE A LINING FABRIC THAT IS THE SAME WIDTH AS THE MAIN FABRIC TO SIMPLIFY YOUR CALCULATION.

For a loose lining, calculate the amount of fabric needed in a similar way, but allow only about 1½ times the basic width for fullness and 2in (5cm) less for the drop.

DIFFERENT TYPES OF SEW-IN LININGS

A lining can be sewn to the curtain fabric all around the side and top edges and then turned out, in the bagging technique (see pp. 62–65) or the side edges of the curtain fabric can be hemmed to the lining. For both methods, the full panels of curtain fabric and lining are made independently first. The header is made after the lining has been attached to the curtain fabric.

SEWING SENSE

When lining a lightweight fabric that doesn't block out light sufficiently, use 'black out' fabric as a lining material. Although usually white, it eliminates light penetration.

PREPARING CURTAINS FOR A SEW-IN LINING

1 Cut the first length of curtain fabric, including the hem and header allowances but not the pattern repeat. Cut the remaining panels, matching the pattern as necessary (see p. 105).

2 Sew any seams, taking ⅜in (1cm) seam allowances and matching any pattern as necessary. Neaten the raw edges and press the seams open.

3 Turn up the bottom edge by 4in (10cm) once, and then again to make a double hem. Stitch a curtain weight into the hem allowance at the bottom of each vertical seam if you wish. Either top stitch or blind hemstitch the hem in place.

FIGURE 1 ADD A CURTAIN WEIGHT IN THE HEM ALLOWANCE AT THE BOTTOM OF THE SEAMS JOINING THE PANELS.

4 On the side edges, turn under the raw edges by ⅜in (1cm) once, and then again to make double hems. Pin the hems in place, attaching a curtain weight inside the hem allowance on each bottom corner if you wish. Don't stitch the hems in place yet.

FIGURE 2 ADD A CURTAIN WEIGHT IN THE SEAM ALLOWANCE AT THE BOTTOM OF EACH SIDE HEM.

5 Working on a flat surface, measure the main fabric from the hem and mark the drop required with pins or chalk across the curtain. Then mark the additional allowance for the curtain header, double the depth of the header tape plus ¼in (6mm), in the same way. Trim any excess fabric from the top edge.

FIGURE 3 CHECK AND MARK THE TOP OF THE CURTAIN AND TURNING ALLOWANCE.

6 Fold the fabric down along the top line and then tuck the raw edge under to meet the first fold to make a double turning. Press and pin it in place.

PREPARING THE LINING

1 Cut enough panels of lining, the same length as the first panel of curtain fabric, to make up the same overall width. Remember you may need a different number of panels, or part panels, if your lining is not the same width as the curtain fabric.

SEWING SENSE

Cut the lining panels straight after cutting the main fabric, while you are still at the cutting table.

2 Piece together the lining panels as you did the main fabric panels. Hem the lining, turning up 3in (7.5cm) once, and then again to make a double hem. Top stitch the hem in place.

SEWING IN THE LINING

1 Place the main curtain panel right sides down on a flat surface and then place the lining on top, right sides up. Position the bottom edge of the lining hem 2in (5cm) above the bottom edge of the curtain hem.

EXPERT TIP

TO REDUCE BULK, OFFSET THE LINING SLIGHTLY SO THAT THE SEAMS ARE NOT DIRECTLY ABOVE THE SEAMS IN THE MAIN FABRIC.

2 Pin the lining to the main fabric along the hem. Then, working up the centre out to the sides and from bottom to top, smooth and pin the lining to the main curtain. Carefully trim away any excess lining along the top and side edges.

FIGURE 4 PIN THE LINING TO THE MAIN CURTAIN AT FREQUENT INTERVALS.

3 Tuck the lining under the side hems and the top turning on the main curtain. Pin them in place. Either top stitch or hand stitch the side hems through the lining.

FIGURE 5 TUCK THE LINING UNDER THE TURNINGS.

4 Attach header tape along the top edge of the curtain (see pp. 94–95), draw up the pleats and hang the curtain.

MAKING A LOOSE LINING

1 Make up the lining panels to give 1½ times the window width and 2in (5cm) shorter than the main fabric curtains. Hem the bottom and side edges.

2 Check the length against the main curtains and fold under a double turning along the top edge. Attach a lining header tape on the wrong side of the top edge (see pp. 94–95 for attaching header tapes).

3 Pull up the cords in the header tape to gather the lining to fit the finished width of the curtain. Position the hooks into the tape at regular intervals and hang them through empty hook pockets in the header tape on the back of the curtain.

FIGURE 6 HANG THE LINING ON THE BACK OF THE CURTAINS. HOOKING ONE TAPE TO THE OTHER.

CALCULATING INTERLINING REQUIREMENTS

Interlinings are sewn into the construction of the curtain. You will need the same width and fullness as the main fabric. However, in calculating the drop, you do not need to add an allowance for a pattern repeat. Once the interlining is attached to the wrong side of the main fabric, both layers are treated as one and can be lined (see p. 132).

ATTACHING INTERLINING

1 Piece together the main fabric in the usual way. Turn and press double hems along the side and bottom edges. Piece together the interlining.

2 Place the main curtain panel, wrong side up, on a flat surface. Lay the interlining on top, wrong side down, smoothing it out from the centre to the edges. Pin the two layers together.

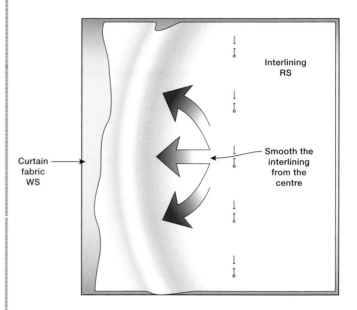

Interlining RS

Curtain fabric WS

Smooth the interlining from the centre

FIGURE 7 PIN THE INTERLINING TO THE MAIN FABRIC, WRONG SIDES TOGETHER.

3 Unfold the bottom hem on the main fabric and trim the interlining to the top fold. Re-pin the hem, securing the bottom edge of the interlining.

WS

Interlining

RS

FIGURE 8 TUCK THE INTERLINING UNDER THE BOTTOM HEM.

4 Tuck the interlining under the side hems in the same way, trimming as necessary. Pin them in place.

ATTACHING LINING TO AN INTERLINED CURTAIN

1 Piece together and hem the lining as explained on p. 130 and then press.

SEWING SENSE

You might find it easiest to work on a large table, stitching the layers together (step 2) and then marking the length of the curtain (step 5) on one section at a time. Then you can slide the stabilized curtain across the table to work on the next section.

2 Working on a flat surface, lay the lining wrong side down on top of the interlined curtain panel. Pin the layers wrong sides together along the centre line. Carefully turn back the lining along the pinned line. Using matching thread, lock stitch all three layers together from the bottom to the top (see p. 16 for lock stitch).

FIGURE 9 LOCK STITCH THE LINING TO THE MAIN CURTAIN.

EXPERT TIP

IF THE LINING IS A DIFFERENT COLOUR TO THE MAIN FABRIC, FIRST LOCK THE INTERLINING TO THE MAIN FABRIC USING MATCHING THREAD AND THEN LOCK THE LINING TO THE INTERLINING USING THREAD TO MATCH THE COLOUR OF THE LINING.

3 Smooth the lining back down onto the curtain panel and pin the next vertical line along the next seam on the main curtain or halfway between seams. Fold back the remaining lining and lock stitch the layers together from bottom to top as before.

4 Continue to the side edge of the curtain. Unpin the side hem. Trim and tuck the lining under the side hem. Re-pin. Return to the centre line and repeat the process, lock stitching the rest of the lining in place. Tuck the lining under the second side hem. Stitch the side hems.

5 Measure and pin along the top of the curtain. Machine stitch through all the layers along the pinned line. Measure and mark the turning allowance on the main fabric. Trim any excess fabric from the top edge and then fold the fabric down to make a double turning.

6 Trim the top edge of the lining, tuck it under the turning and pin in place. Finish the curtain by attaching header tape (see pp. 94–95).

A BEADED OR FEATHER TRIM ADDS A TOUCH OF LUXURY TO CURTAINS.

fabulous
FEATHER-TRIMMED CURTAINS

A SHIMMERING BEAD AND FEATHER
TRIM COMPLEMENTS THE SILKY
STITCHED PATTERN ON THE FABRIC
BEAUTIFULLY AND, WITH THE ADDITION
OF BOUGHT TIEBACKS WITH THE SAME
FEATHER DETAIL, GIVES THESE VERY
GLAMOROUS CURTAINS AN EXOTIC
LOOK. YOU COULD USE THE SAME
METHOD TO INCORPORATE ANY TRIM
THAT IS ATTACHED TO TAPE. THE
CURTAINS ARE LINED AND INTERLINED,
WITH PENCIL PLEATS, TO ADD BODY TO
THE LUXURIOUS EFFECT.

FABRIC CALCULATION

1 Measure the curtain drop (see p. 30) and then add:
- 8in (20cm) for the hem
- double the depth of the header tape, plus ¼in (6mm)
- the pattern repeat (see p. 104).

2 Measure the basic width across the window (see p. 30) and then:
- treble the measurement for fullness
- add an allowance for seams (see p. 30)
- add 6in (15cm) for side hems.

3 Work out how many widths of fabric you need. Then multiply the total drop by the number of widths to give you the total length of fabric (see pp. 30 and 31).

YOU WILL NEED

✓ Curtain fabric (as calculated above)
✓ Interlining (as curtain fabric, minus pattern repeat allowance)
✓ Lining fabric (as interlining)
✓ Deep pencil pleat header tape (add ½yd (50cm) to total width of each curtain)
✓ 2–3 reels of general-purpose sewing thread
✓ Choice of trimming (twice the curtain drop)

✓ Basic sewing kit (see p. 8)

TECHNICAL KNOW-HOW
Attaching interlining (see p. 131)
Making lining (see p. 130)
Using Header tape (see pp. 94–95)

PIECING TOGETHER THE PANELS

1 With the right side uppermost, cut the first length of curtain fabric, including the hem and header allowances but not the pattern repeat. Cut the remaining panels, matching the pattern as necessary (see p. 105).

2 While at the cutting table, cut out the lining and interlining to the same length as the main curtain panel, without the pattern repeat, and to make the same total width as the main curtain.

3 Machine together the main curtain fabric, stitching from the hem to the top.

4 Piece together the lining in the same way. Turn up the bottom edge by 4in (10cm) once, and then again to make a double hem. Press, and stitch the hem in place. Put the lining to one side.

5 Piece together the interlining and then put it to one side.

ATTACHING THE TRIM

1 Lay the main fabric, right sides up, on a flat surface. Mark a line with pins or chalk from the top to the bottom edge, 4in (10cm) in from the leading edge, excluding the hem allowance.

FIGURE 1
MARK THE FOLD LINE FOR THE LEADING EDGE.

Leading edge

Main fabric RS

4in (10cm)

2 Lay the trim tape on the line, with the decorative element toward the raw side edge. Make sure the first decorative element occurs just below the header allowance and the last one is just above the hem allowance. Machine the tape in place.

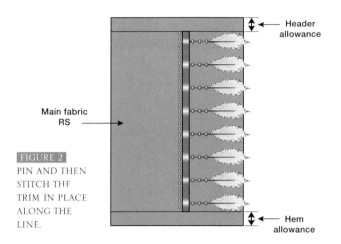

Header allowance

Main fabric RS

FIGURE 2
PIN AND THEN STITCH THE TRIM IN PLACE ALONG THE LINE.

Hem allowance

3 Fold the fabric back, right sides together, over the trim. Machine stitch, parallel to the fold and close to the edge of the decorative element, trapping the tape inside the fold. Press the fold away from the raw edge.

RS

WS

Fold

4in (10cm)

FIGURE 3 MACHINE ALONG THE FOLDED EDGE TO TRAP THE TAPE.

ATTACHING THE INTERLINING

1 Lay the main fabric, wrong side up, on a table with the bottom edge near to you and the outer edge of the curtain hanging down the side of the table. Make sure it is lined up centrally on the table. Lay the interlining on top centrally.

2 You can lock stitch the interlining to the main fabric at this stage if you wish, as explained on p. 131. Otherwise treat the main fabric and interlining as one layer and prepare them for lock stitching the lining through all the layers. Turn up 4in (10cm) on the main fabric once, and then again along the bottom hem. Trim the interlining flush with the first fold of the hem to reduce bulk. Tuck it under the hem and pin the hem in place.

ATTACHING THE LINING

1 Lay the lining, right side up, on the main curtain, positioning the bottom of the lining hem 2in (5cm) above the bottom of the curtain hem. Pin along a vertical line up the centre, securing all three layers together.

2 Fold the lining back from the pins and lock stitch down the fold, following the steps on p. 130 and finishing at the hem sewing line. Continue to pin and lock the layers together in the same way across the section that is flat on the table. When you have locked that section, mark the finished length of the curtain with a row of pins and then mark the line with chalk. Now these layers are stabilized, move the curtain across the table and complete the same processes with the next section.

SEWING SENSE

If you are working on a table, complete all parts of step 1 on each section of the curtain before sliding it across the table and starting on the next section.

3 When you reach the side edge of the curtain, turn in 1_in (4cm) of the main fabric once, and then again for the side hem. Trim the interlining as you did along the bottom hem. Tuck it under the hem and pin the hem in place. Mitre the bottom corner of the main fabric and pin it in place. Using double thread, slip stitch the mitre.

4 Lock stitch the lining down the sides. Turn under the raw side edge of the lining. Pin the lining in place with the bottom corner touching the diagonal line of the mitre on the main curtain. Use enough pins to secure the layers when moving the curtain later. Slip stitch the side edge of the lining to the curtain, using double thread and taking care not to catch the main fabric on the front of the curtain.

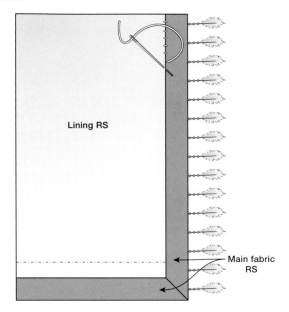

Lining RS

Main fabric RS

GLOSSARY

BAGGING – method of attaching lining to curtain fabric using the sewing machine to stitch around all the edges, leaving an opening/edge for turning

BLIND HEMMING – small stitch that is virtually invisible from the right side

BUTTON FORM – metal or plastic button specially made to be covered with fabric

CASING – channel at the top of a curtain, through which a rod or pole is inserted

CORD TIDY – toggle or plastic shape for wrapping cords to keep the ends tidy

CURTAIN CLIP – clamp that fastens onto curtains and is then fed onto a pole

DRAPES – another name for curtains

DROP – another word for the length of the curtain; the basic drop is from the top to the hem, while the total drop includes any allowances for headings, hems and pattern repeat

EYELET – ring that covers the raw edges of fabric around a hole cut in the curtain header

FIBRE – plant or synthetic substance from which a fabric is woven

FINIAL – decorative end on a curtain pole; there is one at each end

FINISH – surface treatment on a fabric, usually added after the fabric is woven

FLAT FELL SEAM – seam stitched wrong sides together with one seam allowance folded over the other to hide the raw edges

FRENCH SEAM – method of sewing a seam to encase the raw edges of the seam allowance. The seam is sewn wrong sides together first, then re-folded and sewn with right sides together

GOBLET – type of curtain header with pleats forming a goblet shape

HAND/HANDLE – these terms describe how a fabric handles, drapes, folds and creases

HEADER TAPE – also known as drapery tape or curtain tape, this purpose-made stiffening is used at the top of the curtain and is pulled up to form attractive pleats

HOLDBACK – similar to a tieback, this rigid device is fixed next to the window frame and holds back the curtains

HOOK – used to attach curtains to track or rings on a pole

HOOK AND LOOP TAPE – two complementary tapes that can be bought separately or together and used to fix curtains; one tape has tiny hooks and may have adhesive on the back, which can be fixed to a surface; the other, which can be stitched to fabric, has tiny loops that fasten securely to the hooks on the other tape

INTERFACING – layer of fabric, which can be purpose-made and fusible, that adds strength and support to the curtain

INTERLINING – a second layer of fabric that is attached to the main fabric to give extra body and fullness to the curtain fabric

JABOT – also known as tails or cascades; length of fabric draping in folds from the outside edge of a curtain pole

LEADING EDGE – the edge of the curtain nearest the centre of the window

LINING – additional layer of fabric to hide seams and protect main fabric, helps to cut out light and keep in heat

LOCK STITCH/LOCKING IN – catching a tiny amount of one fabric to another using a single matching thread

MITRE – neat finish to corners, stitched at a 45-degree angle

PANEL – a term used to describe a curtain width when more than one fabric width is required, to make up the total width

PATTERN – design woven into or printed on fabric and repeated down the length of the fabric

PATTERN REPEAT – measured from the top of the pattern to the top of the next identical pattern below

PELMET – static, solid window topper, which can be a fabric-covered wooden shape or made with special stiffener

PINCH PLEAT – also called triple pleat, this curtain heading gathers pleats into groups of three, which are stitched together on the front of the curtain

PIPING – a separate raised edging to define the outline. Can be a cord covered with contrast or matching fabric, or a ready-made decorative cord with flange

POLE – usually decorative and visible, curtains are hung from hooks onto the pole rings

RETURN – the right-angled section of the pole or track that attaches the pole to the wall

ROD – similar to a pole, but usually smaller in diameter and hidden by the curtain header

SHEER – translucent fabric

SWAG – decorative swathes of fabric hanging from a curtain pole

TAB TOP – looped fabric tabs at the top of a curtain, through which the pole is fed

TEXTURE – the tactile surface of fabric

TIEBACK – soft ties, made from many materials, that hold back curtains

TOP STITCHING – stitching that is visible on the surface

TWILL – type of weave with a slightly raised pattern, the weft thread goes under two warp threads and then over two warp threads

VALANCE – soft window topper fed onto a rod, track or pole

VOILE – lightweight, translucent fabric

WARP – vertical threads running down the length of the cloth; threads attached to the loom which are lifted and lowered during weaving

WEFT – woven horizontal threads placed under or over the warp threads during weaving

WEIGHTS – lead disks or sausage-like strands of weights used to weight curtain hems so the curtains hang straight

FABRIC SUPPLIERS AND CONTRIBUTORS

With thanks to Vanessa Arbuthnot and Abakhan Fabrics for supplying fabrics for many of the projects (as listed) and to the sterling work from expert contributors who designed and made the curtains. Thanks also to British Trimmings for the tiebacks and to Rufflette for the curtain header tapes, poles and finials.

CHAPTER 1 – *Café curtains by Lorna Knight*

CHAPTER 2 – *Triangular Tab curtains by Lorna Knight*
Fabric: Vanessa Arbuthnott, Out and About Cranberry, Sea Pink (QA 12/11) Windsor antique ivory pole, holdbacks and finials

CHAPTER 3 – *Extended curtains and Pretty Piped tiebacks by Lorna Knight*
Fabric: Vanessa Arbuthnott, Stripe and Wiggle, apple green/sky blue (SW4/7) Pole and finials as chapter 2

CHAPTER 4 – *Dramatic Double Sided curtains by Lorna Knight*
Jupiter rings and solar tape from Rufflette. Two tone glass beaded tiebacks from British Trimmings

CHAPTER 5 – *Shapely Window Dressing by Pen Harrison*
Fabric: Vanessa Arbuthnott, Dandelion Trellis, cranberry/stone (DT12/13) Classic pencil pleat header tape and Press n Drape grip tape from Rufflette

CHAPTER 6 – *Voloptuous Voile curtains by Sue Hazell*
Visions steel pole in matt nickel with fleur finials by Rufflette and faceted ball robe tieback from British Trimmings

CHAPTER 7 – *Voluptuous Voiles with Pocket Surprises by Sue Hazell*
Gun metal pole and Scirocco finials from Rufflette, rectangular curtain pin from British Trimmings

CHAPTER 8 – *Easy Make Triple Pleat curtains by Sue Hazell*
Fabric: Vanessa Arbuthnott Lazy Daisy (LD 16/14) Regis classic header tape from Rufflette, beaded ribbon tieback from British Trimmings

CHAPTER 9 – *Gorgeous Goblets by Sue Hazell*
Goblet header tape, matt nickel pole and Tango finials from Rufflette, Metl mould tieback from British Trimmings

CHAPTER 10 – *A Different View by Pen Harrison*
Gun metal pole from Rufflette

CHAPTER 11 – *Tapered Valence by Pen Harrison*
Fabric: Abakhan Fabrics, Silver Portofino (281483) Track from Rufflette

CHAPTER 12 – *Feather Trimmed Luxury curtains by Sue Hazell*
Apollo light oak pole, Soho light oak finials from Rufflette, beaded feather fringe and tiebacks from British Trimmings

CONTACT DETAILS
Vanessa Arbuthnott (mail order available)
The Tallet
Calmsden
Cirencester
Gloucestershire
GL7 5ET
T: +44 (0) 1285 831437
E: Vanessa@vanessaarbuthnott.co.uk
W: www.vanessaarbuthnott.co.uk

Abakhan Fabrics, Hobby & Home UK
Branches at North Wales, Chester, Manchester, Liverpool, Birkenhead, Preston & Stoke
Shop online: www.abakhan-onlineshop.co.uk
E: enquiries@abakhan-fabrics.co.uk

British Trimmings
PO Box 367, Coronation Street
Stockport
UK
SK5 7WZ
T: + 44 (0) 161 480 6122
W: www.britishtrimmings.com

Conso (for British Trimmings in USA)
6050 Dana Way
Antioch
TN 37013
USA
T: +1 800 628 9362

Rufflette Ltd
Sharston Road
Manchester
UK
M22 4TH
T: +44(0) 161 945 9468
E: customer-care@rufflette.com
W: www.rufflette.com

PICTURE CREDITS
David & Charles would like to thank the following manufacturers for supplying images for the Hardware section (pp24–25):
- Advent Designs
- Byron & Byron
- Integra
- Kestrel

All products from the manufacturers listed above are available at **www.justpoles.com**

ABOUT THE AUTHOR

Wendy Gardiner loves anything to do with sewing by machine. She has been editor and publisher of various sewing magazines for over 25 years and, for the last ten years, has been editor of *Sewing World*, Britain's leading sewing magazine. She has also written many books on sewing, written and presented six DVDs, including *Sew Easy*, *Dressmaking that's Fast and Fun* and *Sew Easy, Soft Furnishings*, and has recently uploaded several more sewing DVD clips on the Internet. She also co-manages isew.co.uk, a website packed with sewing advice, projects and techniques. Wendy is passionate about getting more people to sew and encouraging young people in this fun, affordable hobby.

INDEX